Professional Values & Practice for Teachers and Student Teachers

Second Edition

Edited by
Mike Cole

David Fulton Publishers
London

David Fulton Publishers Ltd
The Chiswick Centre, 414 Chiswick High Road, London W4 5TF

www.fultonpublishers.co.uk

First published 2002
Reprinted 2003
10 9 8 7 6 5 4 3 2

British Library Cataloguing in Publication Data
A catalogue record for this book is available from the British Library.

ISBN 1 85346 931 9

Typeset by Servis Filmsetting Ltd, Manchester
Printed and bound in Scotland by Scotprint, Haddington

Contents

Contributors

Dr Maud Blair is a lecturer at the Open University. She is based in the Faculty of Education and Language Studies and her main areas of teaching and research relate to issues of 'race', ethnicity and gender. She is currently seconded to the Ethnic Minority Pupils Team at the Department of Education and Skills and is co-author of the DfES report, *Making the Difference: Teaching and Learning in Successful Multi-Ethnic Schools* (1998). Her latest book *Why Pick on Me? School Exclusions and Black Youth* (2001) is published by Trentham Books.

Dr Mike Cole is Education Research and Publications Mentor and Senior Lecturer in Education in the Faculty of Education and Sport at the University of Brighton. His most recent publications include the edited collection, *Education, Equality and Human Rights* (Routledge/Falmer 2002) and the co-edited collections *Schooling and Equality* (Kogan Page 2001) and *Marxism against Postmodernism in Educational Theory* (Lexington Books 2002).

Valerie Coultas is Assistant Headteacher in charge of staff development at Selhurst High School for boys in London. She is also Head of the Languages Faculty and has led several departments in London comprehensive schools. As an English teacher and staff trainer, she has a special interest in oracy across the curriculum and pupil-centred learning. She is a regular contributor to the journal, *Education and Social Justice*.

Linda Hurley was a classroom teacher for 20 years before working as a Literacy Consultant for East Sussex LEA. Whilst in this role she wrote *What about Reception?*, a publication which gave practical guidance to teachers on implementing the Literacy Strategy in Reception classes. She is now a Senior Lecturer in Early Years Education at the University of Brighton.

Jeff Nixon began his teaching career in a boys' school in 1972; he then worked in the Community Studies Department of an 11–18 Comprehensive Community College in West Yorkshire, becoming Head of Department and Head of House. Since 1983 he has worked for the National Union of Teachers at the Union's Regional Office in Haywards Heath, initially as a District Officer and now as Regional Officer. The contribution he has made to this book is in a personal capacity.

Joanna Oldham taught secondary school English before undertaking a research post with the British Film Institute and King's College, London investigating the effects of media on literacy. She was lecturer in English Education at King's College for four years where she is currently enrolled for a PhD. Now lecturing at the University of Brighton, her research interests are in social literacies, media and assessment.

Linda Rice began teaching in mainstream primary schools before moving into the special school sector. She has worked in a range of special schools and facilities attached to mainstream schools. Linda worked as a Teacher Advisor for pupils with special needs and is currently a lecturer in Inclusive Education and Special Educational Needs at the University of Brighton.

Dr Krishan Sood (University of Central England in Birmingham) is a senior lecturer in education with special interests in educational management, science education and equal opportunities. In his teaching career spanning 26 years, he has gained a width and depth of experience as a classroom teacher, an advisory teacher and as a lecturer in two universities. He considers it a great privilege to have worked in over 60 primary schools and five secondary schools, small and large, rural and urban, as an advisory teacher in Warwickshire. He has had experience of working collaboratively, in team-teaching situations and in planning, leading and monitoring progress when running INSETs or workshops for a large variety of professionals. He has had a depth of experience of community groups in Warwickshire through his work with the local branch of the race equality council and as past governor of a special school and a large comprehensive.

Professional Values and Practice

Those awarded Qualified Teacher Status must understand and uphold the professional code of the General Teaching Council for England by demonstrating all of the following:

1.1 They have high expectations of all pupils; respect their social, cultural, linguistic, religious and ethnic backgrounds; and are committed to raising their educational achievement.

1.2 They treat pupils consistently, with respect and consideration, and are concerned for their development as learners.

1.3 They demonstrate and promote the positive values, attitudes and behaviour that they expect from their pupils.

1.4 They can communicate sensitively and effectively with parents and carers, recognising their roles in pupils' learning, and their rights, responsibilities and interests in this.

1.5 They can contribute to, and share responsibly in, the corporate life of schools.*

1.6 They understand the contribution that support staff and other professionals make to teaching and learning.

1.7 They are able to improve their own teaching, by evaluating it, learning from the effective practice of others and from evidence. They are motivated and able to take increasing responsibility for their own professional development.

1.8 They are aware of, and work within, the statutory frameworks relating to teachers' responsibilities.

The eight qualities required to fulfil the *Professional Values and Practice* aspect of QTS (TTA 2002)

* In this document, the term 'schools' includes Further Education and VI Form Colleges and Early Years settings where trainee teachers can demonstrate that they meet the Standards for Qualified Teacher Status.

Introduction

'Those awarded Qualified Teacher Status [QTS] must understand and uphold the professional code of the General Teaching Council [GTC] for England.'
Section 1 of *Qualifying to Teach* (Teacher Training Agency 2002)

To gain Qualified Teacher Status, a teacher needs to demonstrate eight qualities, numbered 1.1 to 1.8 in *Qualifying to Teach* (p. 6 and see Figure opposite). The chapters of this book deal with each of these qualities, each chapter considering one of them, although 1.8 is dealt with in the two final chapters (given the breadth of issues covered). The chapter authors have adopted a broad perspective in considering their themes.

In the first chapter Maud Blair addresses herself to 1.1, namely that student teachers 'have high expectations of all pupils[1]; respect their social, cultural, linguistic, religious and ethnic backgrounds; and are committed to raising their educational achievement' (TTA 2002: 6). Blair concludes that while technical competencies are important, they are not sufficient in a diverse, class-based, gendered, multi-ethnic, multi-faith, multilingual society. Teachers, she argues, must be constantly reflective about their practice and must be creative in providing a curriculum that is inclusive of all pupils and that provides social justice in the wider society.

In order to be inclusive of all pupils, it is necessary to 'treat [them] consistently, with respect and consideration, and [be] concerned for their development as learners' (TTA 2002: 6). Thus Joanna Oldham in Chapter 2 addresses the issues of how teachers should treat pupils, and what evidence can be used to demonstrate teachers' appropriate treatment of pupils. Like Maud Blair, Oldham stresses the importance of critical reflection, of a professionalism which is not reduced to atomised components but which incorporates consistency and fairness and an awareness of pupils' personal qualities, particular interests and learning styles, a professionalism which relates to pupils' future adult lives beyond and outside school and which supports their capacity to learn from each other.

Chapter 3 focuses on the TTA (2002) requirement for student teachers to 'demonstrate and promote the positive values, attitudes and behaviour that they expect from their pupils' (1.3, p. 6). Arguing that values are relative, Linda Rice examines the impact of teacher values on pupil experiences and teachers' expectations. Values, she concludes, must be seen in the context of global and national economic and political forces. Although education reflects economic and political processes (intensifying globalisation, market forces, privatisation), it can also challenge them. Teachers and others involved in education can utilise the current government insistence on inclusive education to make demands for an education system that firmly promotes equality and social justice.

In addressing herself to the requirement that student teachers 'can communicate sensitively and effectively with parents and carers, recognising their roles in pupils' learning, and their rights, responsibilities and interests in this' (1.4, *ibid.*), Linda Hurley, in Chapter 4, notes that parent/carer support for schoools is widely recognised as a crucial determinant of educational performance. Drawing on her own research, Hurley argues against seeing parent/carers as a homogenous group, devoid of social class, culture, sexuality and diversity. Often, she concludes, power differentials mean that teachers have the power and parents the anxiety. To reverse this state of affairs, parents/carers should be seen as 'co-communicators', 'co-learners' and 'co-decision-makers' in order for them to have an *active*, rather than a passive involvement in the life of the school.

Like the other contributors to this book, Krishan Sood, in Chapter 5, responds to the TTA requirements in a critically analytical manner. Thus in addressing himself to 1.5 which stresses the need for student teachers to 'contribute to, and share responsibly in, the *corporate* life of schools'[2] (TTA 2002: 6) (*my emphasis*), Sood takes the position that schools should be properly thought of as 'communities' rather than corporations, viewing them as acting as catalysts in bringing the community together. The school, he argues, should help develop community skills, knowledge and capacities regardless of age, gender, disability, social status or ethnic origin.

Chapter 6, also written by Krishan Sood, examines 'the contribution that support staff and other professionals make to teaching and learning' (*ibid.*). Working collaboratively with colleagues in planning, teaching and assessment, inside and outside the classroom, requires professionalism at all times and is essential if we are to provide inclusive education for all.

Requirement 1.7 states that student teachers need to be 'able to improve their own teaching, by evaluating it, learning from the effective practice of others and from evidence'. They also need to be 'motivated and able to take increasing responsibility for their own professional development' (*ibid.*). Thus, argues Valerie Coultas in Chapter 7, an effective teacher is someone who sees himself or herself as a learner. The teacher who is a learner can always contribute to the development of other colleagues. However, it is essential that this is combined with a commitment to teaching and education as a source for building a more egalitarian society, a commitment that will motivate *all* colleagues and pupils.

In order for teachers to function effectively in schools, they need to be 'aware of, and work within, the statutory frameworks relating to teachers' responsibilities' (1.8, *ibid.*). Thus, in Chapters 8 and 9, Jeff Nixon discusses the conditions of service and legal liabilities of schoolteachers. In Chapter 8, he provides a critical analysis of the current conditions of service, in the light of the burgeoning privatisation of education. In the final chapter of the book, Nixon examines the myriad legal requirements to which teachers must adhere, such as the teacher's duty of care, health and safety at work, discipline and detention, and appropriate physical contact and restraint. He concludes with a discussion of legislation concerned with equal opportunities and human rights.

By necessity, a central theme of this book is equality and equal opportunities.[3] If teachers are to have high expectations of and respect for *all* pupils (1.1., *ibid.*), then it is vital that they are aware of the way that social class, gender, 'race', disability and sexuality impacts on pupils' lives. These issues have been pertinent through history (Cole (ed.) (2002)) and they are pertinent now (Hill and Cole (eds) 2001). One of the requirements of TTA (2002) is that those awarded QTS need to 'recognise and respond effectively to equal opportunities issues as they arise in the classroom' (3.3.14, p. 12). This includes 'challenging stereotyped views' and 'challenging bullying or harassment' and 'following relevant policies and procedures' (*ibid.*). In order to do this, it is necessary to understand equality issues *per se* as well as being able to apply them to education (Cole 2002: 3). For example, in order for student teachers to deal with racism in schools, they first of all need to understand what is meant by the concept of racism; to challenge homophobic bullying, they need to be conversant with sexuality issues; to deal with gender differentials in achievement, they need to understand what is meant by gender. In order to deal with social class issues, they need to know about theories of social class and in order to deal with disability issues, they need to be aware of issues of disability rights. These issues are dealt with at length in Cole (ed.) (2002) and Hill and Cole (eds) (2001).

Student teachers also need to know the current state of play with respect to national legislation (see Chapter 9 of this volume for a discussion).

Mike Cole

Notes

1. 'Pupils' is used throughout the book to refer to pupils and students. It is acknowledged that in secondary schools and beyond, the common nomenclature is 'student'. However 'pupils' is used in order to avoid the rather clumsy nomenclature of 'pupil/student'. Where chapter authors are referring specifically to the secondary school, they may use 'student'. In addition, the contributors have all adopted the nomenclatures 'student teacher' and 'teacher education', as opposed to the TTA's 'trainee teacher' and 'teacher education'. This reflects our collective belief that achieving QTS involves much more than mere 'training' (Cole 1999).

2. In the TTA document, the term 'schools' includes Further Education and Sixth-form Colleges, and Early Years settings where student teachers can demonstrate that they meet the standards.
3. A distinction needs to be made between equality and equal opportunities. Equal opportunity policies in schools and elsewhere seek to enhance social mobility within structures which are essentially unequal. In other words, they seek a meritocracy, where people rise (or fall) on merit, but to grossly unequal levels or strata in society – unequal in terms of income, wealth, lifestyle, life-chances and power. Egalitarian policies, policies to promote equality, on the other hand, seek to go further. First, egalitarians attempt to develop a systematic critique of structural inequalities, both in society at large at the level of the individual school (or other institution). Second, egalitarians are committed to a transformed economy, and a more socially just society, where wealth and ownership is shared far more equally, and where citizens (whether young citizens or teachers in schools, economic citizens in the workplace or political citizens in the polity) exercise democratic controls over their lives and over the structures of the societies of which they are part and to which they contribute (Hill and Cole (1999)). While equal opportunity policies in schools (and elsewhere) are clearly essential, it is the view of the contributors to this volume that they need to be advocated within a framework of a longer-term commitment to equality.

References

Cole, M. (1999) 'Professional Issues and Initial Teacher Education: What Can Be Done and What Should Be Done', *Education and Social Justice*, 2(1), 63–6.

Cole, M. (2002) 'Introduction: Human Rights, Education and Equality', in M. Cole (ed.) *Education, Equality and Human Rights: Issues of Gender, 'Race', Sexuality, Special Needs and Social Class*. London: Routledge/Falmer.

Cole, M. (ed.) (2002) *Education, Equality and Human Rights: Issues of Gender, 'Race', Sexuality, Special Needs and Social Class*. London: Routledge/Falmer.

Hill, D. and Cole, M. (1999) 'Equality and Secondary Education: What are the Conceptual Issues?', in D. Hill, and M. Cole (eds) *Promoting Equality in Secondary Schools*. London: Cassell.

Hill, D. and Cole, M. (eds) (2001) *Schooling and Equality: Fact, Concept and Policy*. London: Kogan Page.

Teacher Training Agency (TTA) (2002) *Qualifying to Teach*. London: DfES.

CHAPTER 1

Education for All

Maud Blair

Introduction

The phrase, 'Education for All' became a slogan for 1980s multiculturalism in schools. In Britain, this new ethos, which was heralded by the Rampton (1981)/Swann Report (1985), was a recognition that society needed to face up to the challenges of rapid cultural change that had taken place in the post-war years. The Report (the inquiry was first chaired by Lord Rampton) was an important milestone in the education system. For the first time a major official inquiry highlighted the degree of racism that was affecting a significant number of British children in schools. Although multicultural education had been a feature of many schools in the 1970s, this was the first time that an official report recognised the importance of preparing teachers to acknowledge and cater for diverse cultural needs in the classroom. This led to the setting up in local education authorities of centres for multicultural education and the subsequent implementation of anti-racist training initiatives for teachers. Although many mistakes were made in the name of multicultural education (Cole 1989; 1998) and anti-racist education (McDonald *et al.* 1989) and severe critiques were levelled at some of the training initiatives (see Sivanandan 1985), the Swann Report could be said to have been the first official document to set standards for a more inclusive system of education.

The Standards for the Award of Qualified Teacher Status (TTA 2002) can be seen as building on the Swann agenda.

Under the new Standards, student teachers must provide evidence that: 'They have high expectations of all pupils; respect their social, cultural, linguistic, religious and ethnic backgrounds; and are committed to raising their educational achievement' (p. 6).

There is of course an assumption behind the setting of standards that teaching is a moral enterprise underpinned by a set of commonly accepted truths. Although there are some who would question the validity of such an assumption (for a discussion, see Chapter 3 of this volume) and ask whether it is desirable to set standards and indeed whether there can ever be agreement about what these standards should be, an increasing number of writers and commentators endorse the need to identify a set of working principles which guide teachers and other professionals in their work, especially in relation to work with children (Soltis 1986; Halpin 2000). The relativism that surrounds debates about ethics, values and standards has been dismissed as ignoring the real need that teachers have for guidance in an increasingly complex profession (Campbell 2000). Teachers, it is argued, need to work by a set of common principles not only to safeguard their own professional identities, but in order also to protect children.

It could be argued that standards are particularly important in an ethnically diverse and changing context. The historical experiences of pupils from minority ethnic groups within the British school system would indicate that a code of practice is essential. The last 50 years have not delivered the educational successes on which Asian, black and other minority ethnic families had built their hopes when they left their homes in various parts of the diaspora to come to Britain. At the time of writing, black (Caribbean heritage) pupils and pupils of Pakistani and Bangladeshi heritage as a whole, still straddle to a large extent the bottom end of achievement tables (Gillborn and Gipps 1996; Gillborn and Mirza 2000). The over-representation of black pupils in exclusions from school highlights the tenacity of problems faced by black pupils and the official malaise in dealing with them. The picture is made more complex by the presence of children from diverse refugee and asylum seeking families (Myers and Grosvenor 2001). Then there are local education contexts which reveal difficulties faced by certain white minority ethnic groups such as Turks and Portuguese (Peters 2002).

How are teachers and in particular student teachers to fulfil these requirements in the face of such complexity? This chapter is written for them and is an attempt to provide some pointers as to how best one can translate these abstract requirements into practice. In discussing the Standards set out by the DfES/TTA above, I explicitly accept their validity but do not shy away from acknowledging the difficulties faced by student teachers in their attempt to comply with them as a basis for obtaining their teaching qualifications.

Self-reflection – coming to grips with professional values

The first step in any attempt for the (student) teacher to understand ways of putting the above Standards into practice must needs be a thorough examination of oneself as a teacher – 'who am I, what do I think of children and what do I think of teaching?' Teaching has sometimes been considered a second career option, something one does because other options are closed, or because it fits in with family commitments, or what one does until one has made up one's mind about what one really wants to do (Maylor 1996). There are many, of course, who enter teaching because it is a vocation for them, they are inspired to teach and that is what they have always wanted to do. A close examination of one's motives for taking up teaching as a career is useful in helping the teacher to understand his or her experience of it. Often we look outside ourselves, to external causes when things do not work for us as we would wish. The idea that one is entirely controlled by external forces is disempowering and stymies efforts to address what the real problems could be. Some reflection of why one is in teaching, particularly where a teacher's experience is negative in relation to others in the same environment, might reveal areas of potential change that might help the individual take control of their situation. The thinking might go something like this: 'I came into teaching by default. The result may be that at some level I am not as fully committed as I ought to be. The consequences are that I do not give of myself completely and my pupils[1] can sense this. This is leading to a deterioration in their behaviour and adding frustration and stress to my life.'

This is of course a very simplistic example given only to provide an idea of the direction such thinking might take. It is not assumed that all negative experiences can be traced back to the individual, but that each individual must take responsibility by at least reflecting on where they may themselves be contributing to the situation (Halpin 2000).

The idea that teachers need to reflect on what they do is by no means new (Stenhouse 1983). However, more often than not, this reflection is about methods of teaching and not about the 'being' of teaching. The 'being' of teaching requires an examination of one's values in relation to a range of factors to do with one's world view and whether one is equipped mentally and emotionally for the job.

Haberman (1995) suggests that teachers examine their various prejudices in order to understand how this might affect the pupils they teach. In relation to racism, he discusses a number of steps that he considers to be essential for student teachers.

The first step is a thorough self-analysis of the content of their racism. Those who never get beyond (the denial stage) should not be allowed near children or youth.

The second step is to seek answers to the question of source: How did I learn or come to believe these things? Who taught them to me? When? Under what conditions? How much part of my daily life are these beliefs?

Step three . . . In what ways do I suffer or benefit from my racism?

Step four is to consider how our many 'isms' may be affecting the many issues surrounding what we believe about schools, children and how they learn best.

Step five is the phase in which we lay out a plan explicating what we plan to do about our racisms. How do we propose to check them, unlearn them, counteract them and get beyond them? (adapted from Haberman 1995: 91–2 and cited in Blair and Cole 2002: 71).

In the following sections, I take this last sentence, 'How do we propose to check them, unlearn them, counteract them and get beyond them?' to examine the various elements of the teaching standards given above and on which this chapter is based.

High expectations

It is widely accepted that underachievement in pupils is related, among other things, to the level of expectation the teacher has of them (Blair 2001; Blair and Bourne

1998). How does a teacher check his/her own expectations of pupils? It is important to know the social class, ethnic, gender and special needs profile of one's pupils
and to ask the question, 'What attitudes do I have towards people of this or that
background? What do I know about them? Where did I get my knowledge? On
what are my beliefs and attitudes based? Dependent on age and disclosure, this also
applies to sexuality.

The history of racism, social class, gender, disability and sexuality is imbued with
notions of inferiority (Cole (ed.) 2002). That teachers are no less affected by racist
and/or prejudicial attitudes than other members of society is stating the obvious. In
order to check such attitudes one has to acknowledge them. One method in this
process is to ask the question, What are the common-sense understandings or
stereotypes about this group and to what extent do I take these stereotypes for
granted? Feeding one's guilt about these feelings is at best pointless and at worst
counterproductive. It would be better to acknowledge the presence of normative
and often unsubstantiated beliefs in society and in oneself, and resolve to move on
from there. What in practical terms does that mean? It means getting to know pupils
as individuals and not assuming that their behaviour or performance is somehow
caused by their particular class, gender or minority status. Various aspects of their
experience may be caused by the social and political circumstances or dominant
understandings of 'race' or ethnicity or gender, disability, sexuality and so on,
namely, the way they are positioned in the society, but not by the fact of difference.
Secondly, teachers need to know each pupil well by knowing the circumstances of
their lives and the extent to which these circumstances affect them on a day-to-day
basis. What could be going on in the child's life that is leading to fluctuations in
behaviour or in performance? Thirdly, the teacher needs to set challenges for
him/herself by setting targets for each pupil, reflecting on why s/he has set those
targets for that particular pupil and then devising an individual programme to help
that pupil reach those targets. An important question to ask is, to what extent am I
influenced by that pupil's ethnicity, or gender, or class or disability etc. in setting
that target? To what extent is my action influenced by realistic knowledge of the
individual child and not by 'prior knowledge' of the ethnic group or gender or economic status/social class of the child?

In some cases one's expectations of pupils are influenced by the culture and ethos
of the school in which one works. In one school which had changed from a white
middle-class grammar school to a comprehensive school catering for a largely
working-class Pakistani and Bangladeshi population, the head teacher realised that
the only way to tackle the culture of low expectations of the staff was to create a
system of accountability which made each teacher responsible for the level of
achievement of their pupils. Teachers had to explain to the head of their department
why pupils performed at particular levels, and heads of departments in turn had to
explain the performance of their department to a deputy head. Teachers were thus
forced to look closely at the nature of their explanations and to re-think their
methods of supporting their pupils. This itself became a system of support for the

teachers who were able to identify areas of personal and professional development. Departments that followed this conscientiously experienced a large shift in the performance levels of their pupils (Blair and Bourne 1998). The difference was that instead of teachers blaming the pupils' cultures, or languages or social class positions for their performance, they asked a different set of questions, namely, 'what do I know about this pupil and what am I doing to help and support him or her?'

This practice of looking inwards rather than outwards towards the child and his/her family for explanations of failure or low performance, is an important step in unlearning previously held assumptions. The teacher's concerns must be for ALL pupils so that one is motivated, not by a charitable attitude which in effect renders different ethnic groups 'Other', but by a professional approach which recognises, via honest self-reflection, one's responsibilities towards all pupils.

Respecting the social, cultural, linguistic, religious and ethnic backgrounds of pupils

We often take the meaning of the term 'respect' for granted. Do teachers and pupils share the same meanings? Among the most widely reported concerns of black pupils, especially in secondary schools, is the concern that teachers do not respect them (Blair 2001; Blair and Bourne 1998; Sewell 1997; Wright *et al.* 2000). All pupils wish to be treated with respect, but how do teachers demonstrate this? It is by understanding and then putting into practice the ways in which pupils wish to be respected. A simple questionnaire about what pupils like and do not like about the school will soon reveal many areas in which they do not feel respected. A small study conducted with 200 Year 10 students in a London school exposed widespread unhappiness with the way they felt they were treated by teachers. Statements such as,

'Their body language. It's just rude. And the way they talk to you, man, it's just so rude'.

'It's the tone of voice which they use in front of the whole class.'

'Say you're talking, yeah, and they say things like, "shut up".' (Blair 2001: 54).

These are hardly revolutionary insights. They also apply to all humankind and should be treated just as seriously coming from children and young people as they would do coming from adults. This is, of course, not to deny that pupils are rude to teachers, but what is being underlined here is the importance of teachers always setting the example and being role models for pupils.

Cultural

When the term 'respect' is extended to cultural differences, this poses a particular challenge to teachers and to schools. Misunderstandings can occur very easily, and are an increasing challenge to schools the more diverse the society becomes. Given this situation, what should the teacher do? What is clear is that when parents do not respond to situations in expected ways, for example they respond negatively or do not turn up to a meeting about the behaviour of a child, this is a sign that the school or the teacher needs to delve deeper in order to understand where miscommunication or misunderstanding may have taken place. It is not a sign that the parents are not interested in their children's education. It is often the case that schools do not take the initiative to open up avenues of communication with parents because they feel hampered by language differences, or by a negative interaction with parents from a particular ethnic group, which then translates into suspicion or lack of trust for the whole group. An important question to consider is: What was the tone and manner of the initial communication? Language differences do not necessarily denote different values or different human needs. They may only denote a different way of understanding the same issues, or a simple miscommunication of an issue. Equally, where negative interactions have occurred, it is important that the school or teacher find out what went wrong and re-establish positive channels of communication. It is after all, the school, or it could be the individual teacher, who is providing a service, and not the other way around.

This basic understanding of 'respect' – namely, not operating on the basis of stereotypes, being able to put things right with parents when they go wrong, finding ways of communication which are based on an assumption that parents, whatever their background, are interested and concerned about the education of their children – this is an important starting place before one can hope to introduce initiatives which take into account different cultural backgrounds. Without this acceptance that differences are *different* and not inferior, any such initiatives are not only likely to be superficial, and therefore easy to see through, but likely to be counterproductive and not gain the support of the parents or the pupils. Parents and pupils are the best resource available and once they see that the school or the teacher is interested in them and in their cultures, they will go out of their way to help with time, ideas, and resources (Blair and Bourne 1998). The ethos of the school must therefore be one in which parents and pupils feel comfortable, and have a sense of belonging.

Having established this kind of ethos, it becomes easier to introduce activities that are inclusive of the different cultural heritages of the pupils. In one school, the English department collected folk tales from the children (and this, of course, meant that the parents were involved) and with the rich source of tales from diverse countries, they were able to draw parallels with stories around the world and show the commonalities that exist in humankind and to draw on these parallels in their teaching of literature. It is, however, important not to single out minority students for this information, but to involve all pupils, including those from dominant cultures. People around the world, show, through their stories, that they share the same concerns, the same desires, the same ambitions.

Social

'Social' can cover a number of different areas from social class to peer group cultures. Social class has played a significant part in educational provision in Britain.

From the introduction of mass education in the 1870s to the present day, educational provision has reflected divisions of class in different ways, but generally in ways which have benefited those with middle-class cultural capital (Bowles and Gintis (1976). Social class is, as a result, one of the significant indicators of pupil performance (Hatcher 2000; Hill and Cole 2001).

Social class interacts with ethnicity, gender and other indicators of identity in the experiences that pupils have. An important watchpoint for the teacher is not to assume that ethnicity is the sum total of the identities of pupils from minority ethnic groups. This may appear to be stating the obvious. However, research evidence shows that teachers do sometimes seek remedies for problems based on pupils' ethnicity alone, disregarding other factors that make up the pupils' identities such as their social class position or their age (Blair 2001). This has the effect of blocking the teacher's ability to think through imaginative ways of helping them (Wright *et al.* 2000). There are many areas of disadvantage which working-class pupils from minority ethnic groups might share with their white working-class counterparts and which need to be considered in conjunction with issues of gender and ethnicity. To what extent might a problem be the outcome of poverty or poor living conditions, or domestic disruption? To what extent might the fact of being working class, and black and male be leading to unfair treatment of some pupils and therefore to behavioural and academic difficulties? Individual difficulties have been known to have been attributed to a pupil's 'racial' or cultural background and not to the fact of, for example, racism or adolescence, leading inevitably to mishandling of problems to the detriment of the pupils concerned.

An area of social interaction that has been the subject of much discussion and debate is that of black boys and teachers. Black boys of Caribbean heritage have been and are, at the time of writing, over-represented among those who are excluded from school. Explanations proffered vary from racism (Gillborn 1990, 1995), the strong pull of the peer group on black boys (Sewell 1997), to the over-representation of middle-class white women in primary schools and the absence of black male role models (Abbott 2002).

How is the teacher to understand this and what lessons can be drawn from these various explanations? Again the importance of reflecting on one's own attitudes cannot be overemphasised. Gillborn (1990) writes that black boys are sometimes regarded by white teachers as threatening. The result has been either an unfair level of discipline imposed on black boys, or a fear of reprimanding them leading to an absence of clear boundaries for the pupils in question and consequent deterioration in their behaviour. Every teacher therefore needs to examine his or her fears and anxieties about 'race'. What are these fears and where do they come from? How can they be overcome? How are they affecting relationships in the classroom or in the school?

The peer group is where young adolescents have their identities affirmed and where they feel their sense of belonging confirmed (Cullingford and Morrison 1997; Hargreaves *et al.* 1996). It is a time in a young person's life that teachers need to properly understand. This is particularly important in situations where young people from particular groups feel alienated and/or rejected by the society. The peer group in these circumstances is for young people a refuge and place of safety. It is easy, in circumstances where the peer group constitutes a powerful alternative culture for young people, for teachers to feel that their efforts are in vain, to conclude that the fault lies in the young people themselves and that there is no more that they can do. However, research shows that some teachers succeed with even the most difficult of pupils if one attempts to understand them and their world views, to empathise with what they are going through, to include them in decisions and to take account of their interests and concerns in one's teaching so that what they learn has relevance in their lives (Fine 1994; Ladson-Billings 1994).

Relevant questions to reflect upon here might be: how much do I understand the need for children and in particular young people to establish a sense of their own identity? How is this process manifesting among the young people of (this) school? What is the ethos and social environment of the school and how does it support pupils? What can I do to change things? What is my own relationship with pupils and how far do I attempt to communicate with them in ways that confirm their sense of self?

Linguistic background

Respect is about recognising our common humanity and accepting our differences. The history of racism and of colonialism is a history of hierarchy where people's languages, among other things, were placed both implicitly and explicitly, in order of importance. The languages of colonised countries were inevitably placed in positions of least importance (Blair and Cole 2002). This situation was often perpetuated in British schools where children who spoke one or more languages from non-European countries were in some schools regarded as having 'language problems' whilst the teaching of languages such as German or French to English speakers was considered as improving children's language skills. This often led to children who spoke non-European languages being forbidden to speak their home languages and for these to be considered an impediment to learning English. Research evidence contributed in large part to a re-assessment of this approach. Evidence that use of the child's mother tongue enhanced the acquisition of a second language, helped to shift the perception that these languages were a hindrance rather than a help (Cummins 1991).

However, the acceptance of the logic of language acquisition is not necessarily a sign of respect for other languages. The teacher needs to demonstrate in other ways her acceptance and regard for languages other than her own, and in particular those languages which have been subject to inferiorisation.

Schools use a range of strategies for including the languages of the pupils they teach. At a simple level, schools can display signs and greetings in a variety of languages to reflect the school population. It is simple, and on its own, tokenistic, but is nevertheless appreciated by parents and by pupils who are able to feel welcomed and appreciated by the school. Other displays which depict the histories and achievements of different peoples around the world are also effective and important in challenging normative assumptions about 'Others' (Blair and Bourne 1998). The effective school or teacher goes further to find out about the various displays and what they mean to the communities whose histories they tell and to incorporate this into the teaching and learning process.

Some schools try to be inclusive of both pupils and parents. In the English department of one school, students wrote stories and poetry in their home languages and these were translated and then recited in both the original language and English. Students were also asked to write short plays in both languages so that parents who did not speak English were able to attend performances and understand what was going on. Students' language work was displayed around the school and all languages were seen to be equally valued (*ibid.*).

Displays and other forms of inclusion of diverse languages and cultures are in themselves not enough unless they are accompanied by fundamental reflection and evaluation of one's taken-for-granted assumptions, and pupils are themselves taught to engage in similar processes of reflection.

Religion

At the time of writing, there is a lot of debate in the media and in society about whether or not the State should support Faith schools. The argument against has been that Faith schools are divisive; to support them is to encourage ghettoisation of minority ethnic and religious groups and so threaten social cohesion. The popular belief is that the taxpayer should not be supporting such a move especially in the period post-September 11 and the attacks on economic and civilian structures in the USA. These beliefs are reinforced by social divisions and violent strife between specific ethnic groups such as those that occurred in Bradford and Oldham between South Asian and white people in the summer of 2000. They are also endorsed by political statements about the need to integrate minorities in order to avoid such problems in the future.

At one level, these beliefs constitute good common sense. They also have a wide popular appeal, thus giving them greater legitimacy. But in order to truly learn to respect pupils' diverse religious affiliations, the teacher needs to understand the global and political context in which these ideas are expressed. Had the discussions about Faith schools been taking place in a society in which such schools were unknown and this was a new idea that the public was being asked to support, and through taxation, the arguments could be debated objectively. However, Faith schools have existed in Britain since before the introduction of mass education, and have often been extolled for the positive service they render both educationally and morally to the society. What then is the basis of the objection to more schools of this kind today?

The fact that the schools in question are mainly Islamic (notwithstanding September 11) would have to be considered very carefully as a reason for such objections. The teacher needs first of all to examine the historical relationship between Christianity and Islam, the political context of Islamophobia in the West specifically and in Britain in particular (Commission on British Muslims and Islamophobia 2002), and the hierarchical positioning of religions within the education system and in society generally. Secondly, one needs to ask the questions, In the context of Britain today, what, in principle, do I think about Faith schools regardless of which faith it is? and Now that I understand the debate in its wider context, what position do I take and why? The importance of these questions lies in the practice of thinking critically and reflectively about issues that affect one's attitudes and beliefs and by extension, one's relationships with pupils of different faiths. It is only on the basis of such critical understanding and questioning that one can assess whether one *accepts* and not merely *tolerates* different faiths (Bhavnani 2002), and can properly respond to the needs of pupils of faiths other than one's own.

Commitment to raising achievement

It would probably be unusual to find a teacher who was not committed to raising the achievement of his or her pupils. Why then would such a condition exist in the Standards for qualified teacher status? The probable reason lies, once again, in the racial and ethnic dimensions of academic achievement. Reviews of research by Gillborn and Gipps (1996) and Gillborn and Mirza (2000) have shown the persistence of underachievement among some minority ethnic groups over the years. There is no single explanation for this. Writers have variously pointed to issues of language acquisition, to social class, gender, racism and to an interplay of all these, as significant factors in pupil achievement. An important point made by many social analysts and educators is that teaching is a middle-class profession perpetuating middle-class values and therefore excluding in its processes and underlying assumptions, pupils from working-class backgrounds (Sharp and Green 1984). Furthermore, in a society where the bulk of the teaching profession is white, then the interaction of 'race' and class mediates in a powerful way the relationships between minority ethnic group pupils and their teachers (Sleeter 1995).

The exhortation that teachers be committed to the achievement of their pupils is rooted in an implicit acknowledgement of the role of stereotypes in influencing teachers' beliefs, attitudes and actions. Research shows that such stereotypes affect teachers' relationships with very young children. Connolly (1995), for example, detailed the ways in which six-year-old boys of Caribbean background were labelled and the effects of this labelling on teachers' attitudes towards them. Stereotypes of black men prevalent in the wider society were just as likely to be used against these boys so that they were constructed not only as sexually deviant, but as behaviour problems needing and deserving more stringent control than their white and/or Asian peers.

Individual teachers and schools use many strategies for raising achievement generally and some have developed imaginative and innovative ways to engage their pupils from different social and ethnic backgrounds. Researchers have found that an important method for motivating and encouraging students is to investigate the social and cultural interests of pupils and to incorporate these into one's teaching. Teachers use folk tales, histories, pop and football stars, hip hop music and whatever is topical among pupils or in their communities to bring relevance to points they wish to illustrate in their teaching of various subjects (OFSTED 2002; Blair and Bourne 1998; Ladson-Billings 1995). Important too is the need to understand the barriers to learning for one's pupils. For example, having an afternoon homework club or revision class may be an important strategy. However, unless one monitors take-up of such provision, there is no guarantee that those who need such provision make the most of such opportunities. Boys will often not take advantage of these resources for fear of being labelled swots, or nerds. The teacher or school needs to engage with these fears and find ways of encouraging boys to take up such opportunities. Where particular pupils never seem to take advantage of extra resources provided by the school, it is worth investigating the personal circumstances of the pupil to see whether there are factors in the home or in the school which might be creating difficulties for the pupil. Where a pupil's homework is consistently poor, is it possible they do not have facilities at home for homework? This can be a real issue for refugees or asylum seekers who might live in inadequate temporary homes where a simple item such as a table is a luxury (Virani 2002).

There could be many other factors. For example, is it possible that the pupil is being bullied? Are pupils of Gypsy/Traveller background afraid to come to after-school activities for fear of harassment? Do some pupils live too far from the school to take advantage of what is on offer? Do such opportunities clash with other community or religious activities such as visits to the Mosque? Commitment to raising achievement is therefore about going one step further in one's efforts to make sure that all pupils are given an equal chance to succeed. Providing equality of opportunity is not only about neutral provision of access but ensuring that the outcomes are also fair.

It is becoming increasingly accepted that in order to have a clear picture of whether differential achievement occurs along ethnic, class, gender, disability or other lines, monitoring by ethnicity, class etc. is important. In addition therefore to tracking individual performance, such monitoring provides a picture of group factors and allows the school to see what other value-added factors affect pupils. The Pupil Level Annual School Census (PLASC) through which schools collect and update information on their pupils is a useful tool for cross-checking different kinds of information about a pupil. For example, one is able to take attendance information about pupils from different groups and examine it against gender, SEN and free school meals (as an indicator of social class) in order to provide a more refined picture of truancy in the school.

Free school meals are, however, a crude measure of social class especially as some pupils (especially in Secondary school) who qualify may not take up this service for fear of being ridiculed. It might be necessary therefore, to take, for example exclusion information of Caribbean heritage boys, and set that against free school meals but also against knowledge of the pupil's family circumstances (single parent, poverty, housing, street code or address) in order to get a better understanding of which black boys are most affected by exclusion. A similar exercise can be carried out in relation to information about other groups such as truancy levels among white boys.

Conclusion

Technical competencies in teaching are important but not sufficient in a diverse, class-based, gendered, multi-ethnic, multi-faith, multilingual society. Teachers now need to think in more complex multi-dimensional ways in order to promote a culture of inclusiveness in the classroom and in the school as a whole. This is necessary if one is to fulfil the requirements of QTS set out above. A 'colour blind' approach, that is, an approach that assumes that all pupils are the same and require the same treatment or provision, overlooks the needs and learning requirements of many pupils. On the other hand, an approach which overemphasises differences between pupils, is in danger of creating fixed ethnic or other enclaves which construct groups as 'other' and in the process, marginalises or excludes them. How is the teacher to achieve the balance of perspective that promotes social justice and fairness for all pupils?

This chapter has sought to underline the importance of taking time to think and reflect upon the demands brought about by this diversity. Pupils are not 'the same' because the dynamics of class, gender, sexuality, disability, ethnicity/culture, to name but a few, position people differently and lead to different experiences. The promotion of justice and fairness for all pupils requires an understanding of history, namely Britain's relationship with former colonial subjects (Blair and Cole 2002), with the processes of globalisation and their general impact on different groups around the world, on racial/ethnic, class and gender implications of global as well as local policies and politics (Bhattacharyya *et al.* 2002).

The classroom is often a good starting place for this kind of personal growth and development for the teacher. Faced with pupils from diverse backgrounds, this is a rich source of information and knowledge about the world provided one is open and willing to let go of strongly held beliefs and opinions. It is the inward focus, the examination of one's own world view that is the starting point for high expectations, respect for others and commitment to one's pupils. It can be a challenging place to be but is nevertheless essential. Haberman advises that one examine the source of one's beliefs and prejudices, understand how one came to see the world in this way and then find ways of moving forward in a direction which is always reflective and seeks to take responsibility rather than blame others for problems.

The ability to do this provides a strong foundation for fulfilling one's duties toward pupils from all backgrounds. It might help to strengthen one's feelings for social justice and one's ability to be fair to all pupils in one's care. It also provides a firm basis for thinking imaginatively about teaching and learning and about creative ways of providing a curriculum that is inclusive of all pupils and that promotes social justice in the wider society.

References

Abbott, D. (2002) 'Teachers are Failing Black Boys', *Observer*, 6 January.

Bhattacharyya, G., Gabriel, G. and Small, S. (2002) *Race and Power: Global Racism in the Twenty-first Century*. London: Routledge.

Bhavnani, R. (2002) *Rethinking interventions in Racism*. London: CRE with Trentham Books.

Blair, M. (2001) *Why Pick on Me? School Exclusion and Black Youth*. Stoke-on-Trent: Trentham Books.

Blair, M. and Bourne, J. (1998) *Making the Difference: Teaching and Learning in Successful Multi-ethnic Schools*. London: DfEE.

Blair, M. and Cole, M. (2002) 'Racism and Education: The Imperial Legacy', in M. Cole (ed.) *Education, Equality and Human Rights: Issues of Gender, 'Race', Sexuality, Special Needs and Social Class*. London: Routledge/Falmer.

Bowles, S. and Gintis, H. (1976) *Schooling in Capitalist America: Educational Reform and the Contradictions of Economic Life*. London: Routledge and Kegan Paul.

Campbell, E. (2000) 'Professional Ethics in Teaching: Towards the Development of a Code of Practice', *Cambridge Journal of Education*, **30**(2), 203–21.

Cole, M. (1989) 'Monocultural, Multicultural and Anti-racist Education', in M. Cole (ed.) *The Social Contexts of Schooling*. Lewes: Falmer Press.

Cole, M. (1998) 'Racism, Reconstructed Multiculturalism and Anti-racist Education', *Cambridge Journal of Education*, **28**(1), 37–48.

Cole, M. (ed.) (2002) *Education, Equality and Human Rights: Issues of Gender, 'Race', Sexuality, Special Needs and Social Class*. London: Routledge/Falmer.

Commission on British Muslims and Islamophobia (2002) *Changing Race Relations: Race Equality Schemes and Policies*. London: CBMI with Runnymede Trust.

Connolly, P. (1995) 'Boys will be Boys? Racism, Sexuality and the Construction of Masculine Identities Amongst Infant Boys', in J. Holland and M. Blair (eds) *Debates and Issues in Feminist Research and Pedagogy*. Clevedon: Multilingual Matters.

Cullingford, C. and Morrison, J. (1997) 'Peer Group Pressure Within and Without School', *British Educational Research Journal*, **23**(1), 61–80.

Cummins, J. (1991) 'Inter-dependence of First and Second Language Proficiency in Bilingual Children', in E. Bialystock (ed.) *Language Processing of Bilingual Children*. Cambridge: Cambridge University Press.

Fine, M. (1991) *Framing Dropouts: Notes on the Politics of an Urban Public High School*. New York: Suny Press.

Gillborn, D. (1990) *'Race' Ethnicity and Education*. London: Unwin Hyman.

Gillborn, D. (1995) *Racism and Anti-racism in Real Schools*. Buckingham: Open University Press.

Gillborn, D. and Gipps, C. (1996) *Recent Research on the Achievement of Ethnic Minority Pupils*. London: OFSTED.

Gillborn, D. and Mirza, H. (2000) *Educational Inequality: Mapping Race, Class and Gender*. London: OFSTED.

Haberman, M. (1995) *Star Teachers of Children in Poverty*. West Lafayette, Indiana: Kappa, Delta, Pi.

Halpin, D. (2000) 'Hope, Utopianism and Educational Management', *Cambridge Journal of Education*, **31**(1), 103–18.

Hargreaves, A., Earl, L. and Ryan, J. (1996) *Schooling for Change: Re-inventing Education for Early Adolescents*. London: Falmer.

Hatcher, R. (2000) 'Social Class and School: Relations to Knowledge', in M. Cole (ed.) *Education, Equality and Human Rights: Issues of Gender, 'Race', Sexuality, Special Needs and Social Class*. London: Routledge/Falmer.

Hill, D. and Cole, M. (2001) 'Social Class', in D. Hill and M. Cole (eds) *Schooling and Equality: Fact, Concept and Policy*. London: Kogan Page.

Ladson-Billings, G. (1994) *The Dreamkeepers: Successful Teachers of African American Children*. San Francisco: Jossey-Bass Publishers.

McDonald, *et al.* (1989) *Murder in the Playground: The Burnage Report*. London: Longsight Press.

Maylor, U. (1996) 'The Experiences of African, Caribbean and South Asian women in Initial Teacher Education' (unpublished PhD thesis, Open University).

Myers, K. and Grosvenor, I. (2001) 'Policy, Equality and Inequality: From the Past to the Future', in D. Hill and M. Cole (eds) *Schooling and Equality: Fact, Concept and Policy*. London: Kogan Page.

Office for Standards in Education (OFSTED) (2002) *The Achievement of Black Caribbean Pupils: Good Practice in Secondary Schools*. London: OFSTED.

Peters, M. (2002) paper presented to DfES conference on the collection of ethnic background data and ethnic monitoring, 6 February.

Rampton, A. (1981) *West Indian Children in our Schools*. London: HMSO.

Sewell, T. (1997) *Black Masculinity and Schooling*. Stoke-on-Trent: Trentham Books.

Sharp, R. and Green, A. (1984) 'Social Stratification in the Classroom', in A. Hargreaves and P. Woods (eds) *Classrooms and Staffrooms: The Sociology of Teachers and Teaching*. Milton Keynes: Open University Press.

Sivanandan, A. (1985) 'RAT and the degradation of the black struggle', *Race and Class*, **22**, 1–33.

Sleeter, C. (1996) 'How White Teachers Construct Race', in C. McCarthy and W. Crichlow (eds) *Race, Identity and Representation in Education*. New York: Routledge.

Soltis, J. F. (1986) 'Teaching Professional Ethics', *Journal of Teacher Education*, **37**(3), 2–4.

Stenhouse, L. (1983) *Authority, Education and Emancipation: A Collection of Papers*. London: Heinemann.

The Swann Report (1985) *Education for All: Report of the Committee of Inquiry into the Education of Children from Minority Ethnic Groups*. London: HMSO.

Teacher Training Agency (TTA) (2002) *Qualifying to Teach.* London.

Virani, Z. (2002) Listening to Somali Pupils and Parents: a Research Project. London Borough of Harrow.

Wright, C., Weekes, D., McGlaughlin, A. and Webb, D. (2000) *Race, Class and Gender in Exclusions from School.* London: Falmer.

CHAPTER 2

Concerning Learning

Joanna Oldham

Introduction

Governmental intervention in Initial Teacher Education (ITE) is symptomatic of a more widely perceived crisis of standards in education as a whole (Freebody 1998). The debate about falling standards, whilst hotly contested, is inconclusive and the evidence contradictory (Brooks 1997; PISA 2000). To some extent, the truth of the matter is made irrelevant since the *perception* of a crisis has already been enough to influence the design of curricula. The Teacher Training Agency (TTA) is one such body which has produced new regulations designed to raise standards, in this case for ITE, and their requirements are the subject of this chapter. Although there is great contention about whether or not standards have fallen, with regard to the issues of professionalism and raising performance levels, there is one area of consensus: everybody approves of professionalism *but what exactly is it?* Everybody wants to raise standards *but how is this to be achieved?* The TTA's regulations offer a model of what constitutes professionalism through a set of exemplar performance criteria which outline the TTA's expectations regarding teachers' professional values and practice. This chapter deals with teachers' concern for learning and how this affects their treatment of pupils since the TTA's specifications include the requirement (statement 1.2) that newly qualified teachers (NQTs) will 'treat pupils consistently, with respect and consideration, and are concerned for their development as learners' (TTA 2002a: 4). In what follows, I deal with two questions regarding treatment of pupils. The first concerns how teachers should treat pupils in relation to learning. The second involves what evidence can be used to demonstrate teachers' appropriate treatment of pupils. I begin with a discussion of what constitutes being a professional and the process by which professionalism is learned. I then go on to discuss the TTA's examples of professionalism in relation to treatment of pupils and learning. I continue with a consideration of the broad issues raised by statement 1.2 and their implications for teachers' practice. I conclude by outlining how student teachers can demonstrate that they have met the standards and by examining the nature of the evidence to support this.

What is professionalism?

It is important to begin with the point that it is unlikely that 'professionalism' can be broken down into parts which, when pieced together, saturate the concept of being professional. To demonstrate this, consider a recent description of professionalism written for an audience of beginning teachers by Maguire and Dillon (2001). They write that having the confidence to challenge assumptions about their work, being able to work collaboratively and being able to ask fundamental questions about what they are doing are the features characteristic of a professional teacher, as distinguished from a mere 'deliverer' of a curriculum. Whilst I agree with the significance of the specific issues they cite, I would also want to argue 'professionalism is so much else besides'. In the same text, the authors say that to become a professional teacher, teachers need a feeling of responsibility and control over their work. I would adapt the point thus: teachers need the *authority* to carry out their work; responsibility naturally follows the delegation of control. Since even the newest recruits into teaching are expected to be in control of a host of complex situations, it is not unreasonable to expect them to be professional in the way they execute this control. But what constitutes being professional? Thus we encounter the first problem: that of defining professionalism. Whilst few parties might disagree with each individual example of criteria within the TTA's regulations regarding professional values and practice (TTA 2002a), it seems unlikely that professionalism in its entirety can be reduced to constituent components. Professionalism is greater than the sum of its parts. In the following section I turn attention to the process by which professionalism is acquired.

Becoming a professional

'Craft knowledge' (Brown and McIntyre 1993) is one way of exploring teachers' professionalism and, below, I consider how craft knowledge is acquired and its significance. Brown and McIntyre (1993) define craft knowledge as consisting of 'the professional knowledge and thought which teachers use in their day-to-day classroom teaching, knowledge which is not generally made explicit by teachers and which teachers are not likely always to be conscious of using' (Brown and McIntyre 1993: 19).

Coldron and Smith (1999) say that craft knowledge resides in a person with a 'legitimate teaching identity'. This teaching identity is something you will acquire while you are learning to teach and it results from a transformation you will undergo as you find out how teachers behave and why. Your teaching identity will develop then partly through association with, and observation of, your professional teaching colleagues. Your colleagues will help shape your teaching identity and this process is called social legitimation. Legitimation of your teaching identity is the result of your apprenticeship to a community of practice, that is, other teachers; and through a process which includes practice and apprenticeship and experience and time, you will acquire your own craft knowledge. What accounts of craft knowledge tell us is that professionalism is not achieved by asking student teachers to produce atomistic evidence more appropriate for tick-box assessment. Professionalism is organic and holistic.

Student teachers' practices and professionalism then are informed by becoming members of the teaching community through apprenticeship to experienced teachers. One vitally important point for you to acknowledge is that although professionalism is partly embedded in craft knowledge, learned from association with other teachers, it is clear that existing craft knowledge contains some embedded assumptions, particularly about social practices, that are currently detrimental to learning and need to be challenged. Consequently, the input you receive from your university will be, in part, about equipping you with an understanding of how schools as institutions could *better* facilitate learning. It will be up to you to consider how to translate these ideas into your own practice. Learning to be an effective teacher, then, is not about becoming a copy of the teachers you meet in schools; rather, it is about critical reflection on classroom practice.

Critical reflection is the term used to signify the process of accommodating different ideas in order to gain a cogent understanding of complex situations and it is crucial in learning to teach. If student teachers observe practices which do not reflect the indispensable principle of pupil equality, for example, then they need to consider how the practices could be changed in order to provide equality of opportunity for pupils (see Cole *et al.* (eds) 1997; Hill and Cole (eds) 1999). Although new recruits to teaching are influenced by the contact they have with more experienced practitioners which results in accommodation and ultimately assimilation of the effective practices of the community as a whole, critical reflection is what enables student teachers to identify *which* are the effective practices of their more experienced colleagues. Student teachers learn about professional relationships and concern for learning therefore from observing, considering and reflecting critically on how their more experienced teaching colleagues relate to and treat learners. Consequently, full membership of the professional teaching community is dependent on the change and development within the individual student teacher in accordance with the whole group identity which is situated within the shared purpose of educating learners.

TTA examples of professionalism regarding concern for learning and treatment of pupils

It is important that you acknowledge the TTA's following exemplifications of professional behaviour and attitudes as examples of your broader sense of professional values and practice. You should not interpret the examples as an invitation to construct a one-off task solely designed for the purpose of producing some tangible evidence of meeting the standards. You will, however, be asked to provide evidence in order to demonstrate your professionalism and so, later on, I consider what form this evidence might take and how it can be gathered. Towards the end of the chapter, in order to illuminate the expectations of the TTA regarding treatment of pupils and concern for learning, I discuss these two issues holistically. In the meantime, in what follows, I look closely at each TTA example of professional behaviour.

Scope of professionalism of those to be awarded QTS regarding concern for learning and treatment of pupils

Pupils are more likely to learn if they recognise that their teachers value them as individuals and respond to them consistently. Pupils are more likely to treat others with respect and consideration if their teachers demonstrate such behaviour towards them. Pupils have a range of interests, preferences and attitudes and these will affect how they respond to specific topics or particular ways of communicating. Trainee teachers are expected to take this into account in their planning, teaching and assessment, and to know how they can help pupils to take an active and developing role in their own learning. (TTA 2002b: 4)

Given what I have argued in this chapter, that it is impossible to reduce professionalism to atomised components, you will note that the examples above focus attention only on certain aspects of being professional in relationships with pupils. This does not imply that you needn't be concerned with other aspects which concern relationships with pupils and other factors affecting learning which are not cited above. That being the case, I continue with some of the broader issues raised by the examples above.

Relationships with pupils

Teachers should recognise that some pupils regard them as adults on whom they can depend and rely. As such, they may consciously wish to confide in you or, since children may be less able to conceal things than adults, they may inadvertently reveal personal and sensitive information about themselves to you. The teacher–pupil relationship is not the same as a pupil–parent/carer relationship and it also differs substantially from a relationship between peers because of the inherent power relations which, acknowledged or otherwise, exist between teacher and pupil. A teacher's legal duty of care for pupils complicates notions of confidentiality since the duty of care a teacher has to a pupil will, in certain circumstances, compromise the teacher's ability to keep confidences. The well-being of the pupil overrides any confidentiality principle. (See Chapter 8 for further discussion of this.)

Valuing individuals and their social practices

Education in the broadest terms is different from schooling. Many schools' procedures are self referential in that what schools teach is, to some extent, about the business of schools themselves. The single most important lesson that successful pupils learn in school is how to do school. Thus, successful pupils have learned how to behave for school; they learn what to read, what to write, what to say and how, for the purposes of school. Unsuccessful pupils have not learned how to do school. There are theoretical explanations for this such as Bourdieu's (1984) which suggests that pupils' lives outside school are directed towards goals so different from those of school that they do not understand what schools expect of them and so do not produce it. The particular ways of doing things required by schools are often very different from the ways of doing things required by different socio-cultural groups in the wider society. Outside school, the social practices of different ethnic groups, genders and social classes do not always neatly accord with those within school. Meanwhile, schools as institutions promote and expect only certain ways of doing and knowing; ways which tend to accord with white, middle-class views (Street and Street, 1991). Schools do not reflect the values which underpin the consciousness of wide sections of cohorts of pupils.

Let me offer literacy as an example of whether and how knowledge and skills inside school are the same as those required outside of it. There is an argument that regards literacy as a neutral technology concerned with the skills of reading and writing which is unchanging, no matter what the context. This view is contradicted by another school of thought which maintains that literacy is determined by cultural and social contexts such that 'reading', far from being a homogenous neutral practice, becomes an activity that differs according to the cultural background of the person who is reading. According to this view, there is no one 'reading': instead, it becomes a set of different social practices. There is compelling evidence for such a view. Heath (1983), by investigating home practices of literacy of different groups of pupils, has shown how the function and purpose of literacy is constructed by different social and ethnic groups. So, while some social groups privilege different aspects of literacy, schooled literacy practices privilege largely white middle-class notions of literacy. What might the implications of schools representing only the language of uses of one predominant social group be?

Crucially, such research into social practices offers an explanation for why certain groups under-perform in comparison to others. Heath suggests that the home practices of the middle classes prepare middle-class pupils for educational success, and she claims that the reading and writing practices which vary in other communities are neither valued nor encouraged in schools. One consequence is that teachers (who still tend to reflect white middle-class values) perceive pupils whose literacy practices are more similar to their own to be more able than those whose literacy practices differ. Pupils with literacy practices different from the teacher's are, as a result, perceived as less literate and are then under-assessed by the teacher. This often leads to pupils perceiving themselves to be less able to succeed at school. Clearly, this is dangerous, given that human beings tend to decide how much effort to put in on the basis of how likely they think they are to succeed. The responsibility for this situation is the teacher's however, not least because teacher expectation and pupil success are clearly correlated. This responsibility might seem rather daunting.

Given that it is very likely that teachers are not consciously aware of the extent to which they have lower expectations of certain social groups and value individuals unequally, how should teachers approach teaching and learning? A fundamental starting-point is for student teachers to acknowledge and question their assumptions about the learning strategies which will result in success for their pupils. Student teachers are themselves likely to be successes of the educational system. So only reflecting on your own history is unlikely to help you find out why some pupils do not succeed. The idea that those who fail didn't work hard enough or simply didn't have the aptitude is discredited by the overwhelming pupil-performance data which continues to indicate trends in under-attainment across certain social groups. Recent research (PISA 2000) has attested to the clear advantages of attending schools with pupils from more advantaged family backgrounds since these pupils are three times more likely to attain five or more GCSEs. It would, however, be a mistake to infer from this that wealth is a causal factor in attainment. The data is much more likely to signify the 'cultural capital' (Bourdieu 1977) of individual pupils (where 'capital' becomes a metaphor for different social groups' values and ways of doing things, only some of which are recognised by schools). This extrapolation regarding cultural as opposed to monetary capital is likely to mean that white middle-class pupils have what schools recognise as cultural capital, but that all other groups do not.

Schools' acknowledgement of society's wider demands on people and their social practices which are external to schools is often limited. In terms of becoming a teacher then, you need to become aware of how information, skills and knowledge are transformed by context into a host of vastly different socially situated practices, and to acknowledge the variety of uses to which these will be put outside school by different social groups. It is likely that your university teaching will provide a starting-point for your awareness in these areas. No social practices are neutral however: society accords them different values and it is vital for teachers to be aware of the hegemonic or dominant practices (likely to be those promoted in schools) at the same time as being sensitive to the existence of others. Sensitivity, however, may not be enough. To succeed in schools, pupils also need access to the dominant practices and it is your responsibility to provide this in order to ensure real equality of opportunity.

Responding to pupils as individuals

Teaching is a social activity (social in the sense of being concerned with people) in that it is partly shaped by the particular people in the class and their personal qualities and interests. Evidence suggests that the social make-up of any class will include a range of individuals' different learning styles, interests, preferences and attitudes. For teachers this means that, because pupils have frames of reference different from one another, on a relatively trivial level, what might appear to be a useful explanation to one pupil might not provide clarification to another. Bruner's (1986; 1990) concept of scaffolding gives us a useful rationale for harnessing pupils' particular interests for learning, since he suggests that familiarity and competence in one domain could be used in the acquisition and development of competence in another. Remember that it is axiomatic that learners are better at learning that which they perceive to be useful or interesting to them.

One significant aspect of the teacher's role, therefore, is the ability to explore the particular curriculum subject's relevance and interest for the pupils in the class. This means that you must be able to articulate clear rationales to pupils for learning subject content. You should be aware that your rationale needs to show pupils the relevance and interest of topics in their wider lives, rather than simply pointing out the requirements of the National Curriculum.

To some extent, the TTA's clear acknowledgement that pupils' interests, preferences and attitudes are different is undermined by the existence of a National Curriculum which obliges all pupils to study the same curricula elements during their schooling. Pupils' compulsory education must equip them for the range and variety of directions that they will follow in their adult lives. This is not, however, a call for a curriculum which is only directly relevant to everyday life. The direct relevance argument tends towards the functional over the intellectual when, for most curricula, this presents a false dichotomy. Consider how the different facets of your specialist subject could appeal to a range of different pupil interests, such that there are always elements of any lesson in which all pupils can engage enthusiastically.

Treating pupils with respect and consideration

There is a tension, unacknowledged by the TTA, between the ideas of fairness on the one hand (treating all pupils in the same ways) and inclusion on the other (treating some pupils in particular ways for particular reasons) which, understandably, student teachers may struggle with in practice. It is, however, a worthy aim to respect and consider pupils and to value them as individuals equally. It is also vital to have similar expectations of pupils with regard to conduct, a term which I use here to include work and behaviour in class.

Let us turn to the issue of school work. It would appear clear that all human achievement, if plotted on a graph, would result in a normal distribution curve (sometimes called a bell-shaped curve) which shows that a small minority of performance falls at the extremes. Very few people will perform at the lowest levels and, similarly, very few will perform at the highest levels: the vast majority of performance will fall in the mid-range, though there will be differences between individuals here too. This variation demonstrates what we already know from the application of common sense: that, while genuine extremes are rare, we are all different from each other. With regard to classes of pupils, variation in their performance will still occur (even in setted classes, demonstrably, pupils are not the same). Valuing all individuals equally involves understanding that some pupils (in fact, half of them) will always perform beneath any norm and that it would be therefore catastrophic to concern oneself only with the education of pupils who are above average: such pupils will constitute only 50 per cent of the school population.

What we also know about human achievement is that it is possible for an individual to be good at one thing and not at another. These two factors about achievement combined suggest that, in classroom situations, teachers should offer an equality and opportunity and, also, be prepared to support those pupils whose performance falls below anticipated norms such that it is possible for their attainment to be raised. Teaching pupils what they need to learn such that their attainment is raised is what marks genuine equality in the classroom. Your preconceptions and prejudices about which pupils are likely to produce good work might appear to be justified by pupil performance. Preconceptions and prejudices, however, they remain. Teachers must also have sufficiently flexible expectations of different pupils and not overly prescribe the allocation of pupils to differentiated tasks in order to avoid pupil performance becoming a teacher-fulfilled prophecy.

Valuing individuals and responding to them consistently therefore manifests itself in the practice of a teacher who, while acknowledging that performance will differ, does not rigidly predict which pupils will be able to engage with particular tasks, nor how successfully. A fair teacher also expects equal effort and input from all pupils, which means making the same demands of all pupils. The fact that a pupil produces a good piece of work doesn't mean that he or she has made much effort. Your job is to stretch all pupils, including the most able, so that they all improve and develop. Regarding both school work and behaviour, in order that pupils understand teachers' expectations of them it is important first for teachers to determine that their expectations are reasonable; second, for teachers to be explicit to pupils about what the expectations are; and third, for teachers to reinforce their expectations consistently.

Acknowledging learning as a individualised process

Learning is interactive: it requires that the learners and the teacher be involved in an active dialogue about the work. This means that it is not enough to construe the teaching process as the space in which teachers recount their knowledge to pupils who, merely by listening, simply absorb the information. Learning is an active process and relates not only to knowledge of facts, but also to application of ideas. The latter requires understanding, whereas the former hinges on the more limited skill of recall. To encourage pupils' understanding, teachers need to provide a range of learning experiences to pupils in classroom situations. Vygotsky's influential theory (1962; 1978), that pupils learn in a social context through spoken interaction with others (including not only the teacher but also other pupils), is known as the Zone of Proximal Development (ZPD). ZPD refers to learning taking place as a result of interaction with another person. Vygotsky recognised that language does not only represent a tool for display of learning, but that it is also elemental in the learning process itself. Such theories call into question the wisdom of classrooms where learning is individual and conducted in silence. Tharp and Gallimore (1988) claim that the nature of ZPD is socially situated and varies according to the society from which the learner comes. In so doing, their finding makes a clear case for teachers making pupils' formal and informal learning environments more similar through the incorporation of a wider range of social practices. The danger of not doing so is that pupils whose practices outside school differ from those in school will be hindered in their formal learning by the barrier of schooled practices, practices schools tend not to acknowledge but regard as neutral.

Comment on the TTA's examples of professionalism

Recent governmental emphasis on standards in education has tended to focus attention only on that which is measurable, e.g. skills, and that which can be reduced to atomistic competencies for the purposes of testing. Although born of a (legitimate) desire to make teaching and teachers more rigorous and more accountable, this drive towards hyperspecification of criteria in initial teacher education, reminiscent of similar moves in wider educational assessment issues, could actually undermine rather than strengthen professionalism. If student teachers focus too much attention on collecting evidence related to the specific practice the TTA offers as examples of professional behaviours, they could be missing the point: that the concept of 'professionalism' cannot be saturated by describing *all* professional behaviour. That being the case, you should regard the TTA's examples, not as a checklist but rather, as exemplifications of behaviours from which *wider inferences* about your appropriate relationships with pupils can be reliably made. Such an approach prevents expectations regarding professional relationships and professionalism from being reduced to a handful of (disputed) principles.

What informs the current limitations, that is, the factors which determine what aspects will be assessed and which will not, is to a certain extent, pragmatism. What can be measured is assessed and what can not be measured is not. Wiliam and Black (1996) talk about the potential consequences of this insofar as what is (and what is not) assessed communicates values to those being assessed. Moreover, they argue that the consequences of assessment can be seen in terms of the curriculum and what gets taught. What are the implications of this for professionalism? If what is tested is informed solely by what is testable, this might lead to student teachers prioritising the assessable elements of the domain alone and concentrating only on those aspects of their practice which generate evidence, which would result in a narrowing of the curriculum (conscious or otherwise). This point raises the question of who will be responsible for undertaking the assessment of student teachers and how it will be done and I deal with this later in the chapter. In the meantime, in the next two sections respectively, I want to discuss how professional teachers treat pupils and indicate how teachers are concerned with learning.

How should teachers treat pupils?

Having examined the TTA's examples of professional behaviour, I now specifically address the issue of how teachers should treat pupils. Research conducted into how classrooms operate suggests that boundaries and relationships are in a constant state of negotiation between teachers and pupils. This means that no one pattern of behaviour or set of preconceived responses can be unproblematically applied to every situation. This is a potential source of worry for beginner teachers who could be forgiven for wanting to know everything they need to know before they set foot in a classroom! This clearly isn't possible when much of learning about teaching is learnt by translating your observations of, and critical reflections on, other teachers' teaching into your own practice which will develop over time.

Earlier, I examined how teachers acquire craft knowledge which could be interpreted as a framework for decision-making more flexible than any simple rule or regime (either of which are likely to be inapplicable in totality). Acquisition of craft knowledge is dependent on observation and critical reflection: observation of one's own practice and that of others and, more importantly, critical reflection on both. It is difficult to overstate the significance of observation of, and critical reflection on, other teachers in learning how to teach. If you're not learning anything, it is likely that you are not looking or reflecting carefully enough. Student teachers need to come to an understanding about why experienced teachers do things in the ways they do. This involves acknowledging the complex range of factors experienced professionals are taking into consideration when they treat pupils in certain ways. Student teachers should also, however, consider alternate ways of doing things which may have a greater appropriateness for pupils and their education. Inevitably, student teachers will not always see examples of best practice since teachers' performance is, like all endeavour, normally distributed and will contain elements of both good and bad. Whilst ensuring you are tactful about your responses to other teachers' practice, it is useful to consider why some lessons you observe haven't gone as well as they might have done.

As a teacher, you should model the sorts of courteous and polite conduct you expect from your pupils. A paramount concern for student teachers at the beginning of their practice is classroom management and pupil behaviour, anxieties about which sometimes threaten to undermine the teacher's resolve to be courteous and polite. An orderly classroom is needed but you can't afford to obtain one at the expense of healthy working relationships with pupils. Watch to see the host of techniques experienced teachers use in managing behaviour before they are obliged to implement schools' formal behaviour sanctions. Some of these techniques can be very subtle. Techniques which do not rely solely on punitive measures, for example use of good humour, can be the most effective.

How should teachers show concern for learning?

Although there are different ideas about the purpose of schools, all of them place fundamental significance on the value of learning. In the present context, schools are increasingly entrenched in the education culture of league tables, parental choice and OFSTED inspections with the power to close schools. One ironic result of this is that attention is sometimes forced away from the issue of learning and focused on results. Measurement has, to some extent, become the end rather than the means in education. In classrooms, one potential consequence of the results-oriented pressure on teachers is that assessment of pupils happens more often in order that pupils' development can be shown. Before a more detailed exploration of assessment's place in the learning process, I want to clarify the difference between teaching and learning. If the learner hasn't learnt anything, can what the teacher is doing accurately be described as teaching? A teacher can be operating the *procedures* of teaching, for example, talking to the pupils, but if learning has not occurred, there is an argument for saying that no teaching has taken place. Teaching and learning then are mutually dependent.

Learning is conspicuously different from the demonstration of *prior* learning. If, for example, a teacher asks a pupil in a music classroom to sit at the piano and play, the pupil will be demonstrating that which he or she could already do before entrance into the classroom. This is demonstration of prior learning and not learning *per se*. Teachers, because they are obliged to assess pupils' learning, do provide occasions for pupils to demonstrate what they can already do but this is an activity separate from learning and an issue I return to later. For student teachers, in the first instance, it is vital to know how learning occurs. Returning to my example of the pupil playing the piano in class, if the teacher listens to the pupil's demonstration of *prior* learning and forms an opinion about how well the pupil is playing, then learning is what happens *after* this point. Let me explain how. If the teacher identifies the next step for the pupil's development in piano playing and gives advice to the pupil about how to make that next step, and if the pupil uses the teacher's advice and plays the piano better the next time, then the teacher has taught and the pupil has learned.

Learning then is intimately linked to a certain type of assessment sometimes called formative assessment or, more recently, termed 'assessment for learning'. This type of assessment is different from the sort (called summative assessment) that simply allows the teacher to find out what the pupils can already do. Summative assessment has no effect on learning. If our piano-playing student plays the piano for the teacher who assesses the performance and that is the end result, then this assessment is summative and has not, in itself, had an effect on the pupil's level of performance. Assessment for learning's intention, however, is to *improve* performance. This is achieved through the direction the teacher gives to the pupil about how to achieve the next developmental step required by his or her current performance in order to raise it from one level of performance to the next, higher level. The crucial factor in this process is the teacher's communication to the pupil known as 'feedback'.

Learning does not automatically result from all feedback: it is the *quality* of the feedback which is significant in determining whether learning will occur. Feedback which tells a pupil to 'be more analytical' is only useful if the pupil knows what being more analytical means and understands *precisely* what steps to take to make the piece of work on which feedback is being given more analytical. It has been suggested (Wiliam and Black 1996), that if a pupil knew what being more analytical looked like, he or she would probably have been analytical in the first place. The feedback has to be understandable by the pupil. If a question set for pupils to answer is 'what matter produces a chemical that causes bubbles to be formed in hydrogen peroxide solution?' (answer: living cells), and a pupil asks for assistance, informing the pupil that a leaf will cause bubbles but a stone will not, only gives the pupil an example. It will not help the pupil to answer another question about whether matter of a different type is likely to have the same bubbling effect unless the pupil already knows that the teacher's example of a leaf is offered *as an example of a living cell*. The teacher can accept the credit for a pupil's improvement in performance only if the pupil has used the teacher's feedback. Feedback, then, has to be tailored to the individual pupil's capabilities, existing knowledge and understanding. This is where teachers' knowledge of the pupil's performance through summative assessment is useful in assisting learning: it helps the teacher know what kind of feedback is appropriate for the pupil.

How do teachers make these assessments for learning which, as I have indicated above, are crucial to the learning process? Teachers' assessments (and subsequently, their feedback) come not from criteria relating to the task pupils are engaged in (e.g. use of quotations in a literary essay) in a verbal description (e.g. 'skilfully used') but by reference to their wide understanding of quality. Teachers have an understanding of quality in their curriculum discipline because of the wealth of knowledge and experience they have of their subject. They know what a good translation in languages looks like; they know what a good mathematical proof looks like; they can recognise an effective poem etc. Teachers' own subject knowledge proficiency is so well developed that they know the full (unwritten) criteria of their subject: the task is to share this information with the learner.

The knowledge of the expert (in this instance, the teacher) comes about through experience, apprenticeship and tutelage. The novice's knowledge (the pupil's) is acquired in the same way as the expert's:

> Knowledge of the criteria is 'caught' through experience, not defined. It is developed through an inductive process which involves prolonged engagement in evaluative activity shared with and under the tutelage of a person who is already something of a connoisseur. (Sadler 1989)

So, in order to improve, pupils must be given both a wide range and multiple classroom experiences of your curriculum subject and feedback relating to their performance. In addition, pupils must be given multiple opportunities to experience and practise certain aspects of the subject, say, writing essays for Humanities. For learning to occur, when the teacher sets the task, he or she needs to explain clearly what is expected from the work. As an example, take the task to be an essay and the expectation to be pupils' use of quotations from sources in the essay. In addition to experience and clear expectations about the task, pupils also need an opportunity to redraft their work in the light of the teacher's feedback. The feedback should be in response to a first draft and directed towards improving the pupil's second draft.

At the point of feedback, the teacher might want to discuss with the pupil *how well* he or she has used quotations in the first draft of the essay, or, if the pupil's quotations are already very good, the teacher might direct the pupil to improve a different aspect of the work. To develop my example of how teachers facilitate learning, assume that the teacher wants the pupil to improve the way in which quotations were used in the first draft of the essay. It is not enough for the teacher to say 'your use of quotations needs to be better': this does not tell the pupil what aspects of quotation use needs to be better, nor how this can be done. *It is your job to show the pupils how.* It is not enough either to present examples of work to the whole class and inform the pupils which example was excellent and which merely satisfactory. Teachers must also explain the criteria by which they deem one pupil's essay 'excellent' and another's 'satsifactory'. Thus teachers need to be able to explain precisely what work which is excellent contains. This involves not only giving the information that 'quotations are used very skilfully in this essay', but also an explanation of exactly what makes the example skilful and how a skilful example differs in nature from a weaker example.

To facilitate learning, the teacher needs to ensure the learner has the following: first, an understanding of the full criteria against which work is assessed; secondly, some sense of the aspired level of performance; and thirdly, an ability to *compare* their actual levels of performance to the higher, aspired level of performance. Without these things, 'students' efforts in production are likely to contain elements of random trial and error' (Sadler 1987). So taking those three things in turn, firstly, how do teachers share criteria with learners? By showing pupils how the criteria apply to specific examples of pupils' work in concrete terms. Secondly, how do pupils learn about the level of performance above? By seeing examples and having the teacher explain precisely how and in what ways higher performance is different. Thirdly, how do teachers enable pupils to compare their own performance to the higher level? By involving pupils in the evaluation of their own work. Once pupils have this knowledge and understanding, they are also able to evaluate each other's work. Looking at other pupils' work *in the light of* the teacher's feedback raises achievement (Wiliam 1998).

Teachers' concern for learning is shown through the *quality* of the feedback they give to pupils and the number of opportunities they provide for pupils precisely for the purpose of evaluation and feedback.

Demonstrating meeting the standards

If the standards the TTA has proposed are intended to have a gatekeeping function whereby only those student teachers who can demonstrate professional competence will be granted admission to the profession, then your professionalism must be assessed. This final section of the chapter considers what will be assessed, when and by whom and it aims to clarify the nature of evidence that will suggest you have met the standards.

Professionalism is something that should underpin and inform all of the inter-actions you have with pupils. This chapter has drawn your attention to polite and courteous relationships with pupils and to a consideration of the learning process. The task for student teachers is to combine both sets of practices such that pupils' learning is conducted in a supportive atmosphere. Such an atmosphere is created by the teacher's implicit and explicit expectations. Pupils receive messages about what the teacher's expectations are, not only from what they say, but also from more subtle clues including the tone of voice the teacher uses, facial expressions and body language. In addition, the feedback the teacher gives and the comments the teacher makes about the pupil's work give the pupil an impression of how suc-cessful the teacher thinks the pupil's work has been. The teacher needs to be careful not to undermine pupils' confidence, but just as importantly, not to suggest that there is nothing more for the pupil to learn. For this reason, it is important to be clear about what minimum expectations of pupils' attainment are and as your craft knowledge develops, you will become clearer about what appropriate levels of attainment for different age groups and different individuals are. Teachers tend not to have a maximum expectation: they rightly don't want to set a ceiling on pupil attainment.

Being professional is something that student teachers should work towards in every aspect of their practice. As I have already suggested, it is something that devel-ops over time. Professionalism in teaching is an underpinning concept and, as such, quantitatively and qualitatively different from a person's ability to behave profes-sionally for a given occasion. That being the case, your professionalism will be observable at all times, and by all of the people (including the pupils) with whom your school practice brings you into contact. The evidence of your professionalism will be also reflected in the documentation that ITE generates. Evidence of *your* developing professionalism will thus be observable during the lessons in which you participate (either as observer or teacher) and in your general conduct in the school. The people who will assess your professionalism on this evidence will be staff with responsibility for your school practice and your university tutors. Your professional concern for pupils as learners will be particularly evident in your lesson planning as well as the actual lessons you teach. Reflect upon your planning and teaching and ask whether you have introduced your task and its criteria clearly, whether you have provided an opportunity for redrafting work in response to feedback you have given. If not, pupils will not be learning. Your teaching cannot be separate from pupils' learning, it must be integral.

What this chapter has attempted to do is to share the criteria with you, the learner. Your task now is to apply the concept of professionalism to actual exam-ples you see of it and to compare your own professional conduct with good exam-ples amongst your professional colleagues. You are not alone in this process: it is the job of both your school- and university-based tutors to give you the crucial feedback necessary for helping you shape your own, individual professional teach-ing identity.

References

Bourdieu, P. (1977) *Outline of a Theory of Practice*. Cambridge: Cambridge University Press.

Bourdieu, P. (1984) *Distinction: A Social Critique of the Judgment of Taste*. Cambridge, MA: Harvard University Press.

Brooks, G. (1997) 'Trends in Standards of Literacy in the UK 1948–1996'. Paper given to British Educational Research Association, York.

Brown, S. and MacIntyre, D. (1993) *Making Sense of Teaching*. Buckingham: Open University Press.

Bruner, J. (1986) *Actual Minds, Possible Worlds*. Cambridge, MA: Harvard University Press.

Bruner, J. (1990) *Acts of Meaning*. Cambridge, MA: Harvard University Press.

Coldron, J. and Smith, R. (1999) 'Teachers' Construction of their Professional Identities', *Journal of Curriculum Studies*, **31**(6), 711–26.

Cole, M., Hill, D. and Shan, S. (eds) (1997) *Promoting Equality in Primary Schools*. London: Cassell.

Freebody, P. (1998) *Assessment as Communal Versus Punitive Practice: Six new literacy crises* AILA Virtual seminar series www.education.%20uts.edu.au

Heath, S. B. (1983) *Ways with Words: Language, Life and Work in Communities and Classrooms*. Cambridge. Cambridge University Press.

Hill, D. and Cole, M. (eds) (1999) *Promoting Equality in Secondary Schools*. London: Cassell.

Hill, D., Cole, M. and Williams, C. (1997) 'Equality and Primary Teacher Education', in M. Cole, D. Hill and S. Shan (eds) *Promoting Equality in Primary Schools*. London: Cassell.

Maguire, M. and Dillon, J. (2001) *Becoming a Teacher: Issues in Secondary Teaching*. Buckingham: Open University Press.

PISA (2000) *Knowledge and Skills for Life*, www.pisa.oecd.org

Sadler, D. R. (1987) 'Specifying and Promulgating Achievement Standards', *Oxford Review of Education*, **13**(2), 191–209.

Sadler, D. R. (1989) 'Formative assessment and the design of instructional systems', *Institutional Science*, **18**(2), 199–244.

Street, B. and Street, J. (1991) 'The schooling of literacy', in D. Barton and R. Ivanic, *Literacy in the Community*. London: Sage, pp. 143–66.

TTA (2002a) *Qualifying to Teach: Professional Standards for Qualified Teacher Status and Requirements for Initial Teacher Training*. London: DfES.

TTA (2002b) *Handbook Accompanying the TTA (2002) QTT Guidelines*. London: DfES. http://www.canteach.gov.uk/community/itt/requirements/index.htm

Tharp, R. and Gallimore, R. (1988) *Rousing Minds to Life*. Cambridge: Cambridge University Press.

Vygotsky, L. S. (1962) *Thought and Language*. Cambridge, MA: MIT Press.

Vygotsky, L. S. (1978) *Mind in Society*. Cambridge, MA: Harvard University Press.

Wiliam, D. (1998) 'Enculturating Learners into Communities of Practice: Raising Achievement Through Classroom Assessment'. Paper to European Conference on Educational Research, Ljubljana, Slovenia, September.

Wiliam, D. and Black, P. J. (1996) 'Meanings and Consequences; a basis for distinguishing formative and summative functions of assessment?', *British Educational Research Journal*, **22**(5), 537–48.

CHAPTER 3

Promoting Positive Values

Linda Rice

'A rising tide lifts all boats.' (Tim Shriver)

Introduction

Those awarded Qualified Teacher Status (QTS) must understand and uphold the professional code of the General Teaching Council for England by demonstrating the Professional Values as outlined in Section 1 of *Qualifying to Teach: Professional Standards for Qualified Teacher Status* (TTA 2002a). They must be able to 'demonstrate and promote the positive values, attitudes and behaviours that they expect from their pupils' (TTA 2002a: 1.3). Examples of the values that can be expected are: respect for other people; a positive attitude towards learning; respect for cultural diversity; care for the environment; and social responsibility (TTA 2002b: 4).

Values have been defined in many and varying ways, and this chapter uses Halstead and Taylor's (1996) definition of values as simply the principles and fundamental beliefs which act as general guides to behaviour and as points of reference in decision-making.

I set out here to discuss some of the formidable and controversial issues that arise when considering professional values and the role of the teacher. There are two inherent assumptions in the Standards. First, that teachers see it as their role to influence the development of pupils' values and secondly that 'children's values will be influenced, consciously or otherwise by the example set by their teachers in their relationships, attitudes and teaching styles' (Halstead and Taylor 2000: 177).

I would also wish to stress the importance of teachers and pupils developing critical thinking and an understanding of a variety of ways of interpreting the world. This allows a conception of values as relative rather than absolute.[1]

Much of the influence that teachers have upon pupils might best be described as indirect, that is to say, it happens without pupils or teachers being consciously aware of it. 'The indirect moral influence on children is deeply embedded in the daily life of the school, either within normal teaching activities or within the contingent interactions at classroom level' (Halstead and Taylor 2000: 177). In the classroom, this could be, for example, verbal and subtle non-verbal behaviours, more obvious behaviours such as encouraging prompt arrival to lessons, careful differentiation of lessons and sensitive marking of work and more easily observed differences in teaching styles. This picture is complicated by the fact that these teacher behaviours will be interpreted differently by different pupils.

Teachers have a responsibility to clarify their own values and attitudes, to articulate them, in order to be able to enter into reasoned debate when confronted with opposing views. Teachers often have difficult professional choices to make and understanding their own values may provide them with some rationale for judgements and decisions. Reflecting on their practices may also give them some indication or insight into what it is that they value. Values need to be examined in terms of the experiences of pupils, of teachers' expectations of pupils, and wider economic and political factors that influence the 'what' and the 'why' of teacher values. The role of the teacher as critical transformative intellectual should not only resonate with all members of the school community, but should extend beyond, in the local community, in teacher unions and other associations, and in the world at large. Learning to teach is a complex and lifelong process. It is much more than the ticking of boxes that demonstrates achievement of competencies. It is also more than a set of technical skills.

The development of professional values is dynamic and complex. It is ongoing and deeply influenced by one's personal history long before one's initial professional teacher education even begins. Unravelling this web poses an interesting and exciting task. This chapter sets out to raise awareness of some of the obvious and clearly defined, as well as some of the hidden agendas within the topic. It is in three sections: pupils' experiences, teacher expectations and economic and political factors. All of these impact upon teachers' values and thus, in turn, upon the teaching and learning that goes on in classrooms.

Pupils' experiences

Pupils experience school differently depending on, for example, their age, gender ability, social class, ethnicity, and how they interact with their teachers and their peers. We know that an individual's values change over time and that their development is a lifelong process (Cairns 2000). Our values are thus constructed in a particular social context and climate. They are forged in the struggle between conflicting social forces in any given society. Out of these conflicting social forces collective values and identities may be formed.

> Gender, race, ability, class 'academic' or 'non-academic', anti-school or pro-school may be the salient characteristics of one's identity, but only when school structures and the nature of the school's social mix push that feature into social prominence. (MacBeath and Mortimore 2001: 13)

Values are thus socially constructed, adopted and adapted in the contexts in which we grow up. The influences of home and community and peer group are clearly significant. Pupils may be involved in activities out of school, e.g. leisure and religious groups. Values encountered in taking part in such activities will be both explicitly and implicitly articulated. 'Some of these interests serve to promote not only personal and social development, but also a growing awareness of being a member of several communities with differing values' (Taylor 1996: 134). For many pupils, community language and beliefs are central to their identity and the way they live. Their awareness of the differences that exist between themselves and their peers may give cause for concern or even conflict. Clearly, this has relevance for teachers.

Schools and teachers have a significant role in empowering pupils to manage conflict and difference. In terms of context, school plays a significant part in most children's formative years, and will inevitably have an impact upon the individual's developing value set.

Schools vary enormously. They may be rural, urban, inner city, Faith, fee-paying, state, Beacon, selective or comprehensive. They may serve predominantly mono-cultural or multicultural communities. Schools are increasingly requested to artic-ulate in their policies their underlying values, and to reflect on the way that the life of the school may contribute to the development of the pupils' values and attitudes ' (Halstead and Taylor 2000: 176). All will have values enshrined within policies that are likely to differ in a minor or major way from each other. The type of school one goes to can profoundly effect one's values and indeed life chances. For example, where selection still exists, pupils going to primary school experience selection at age 11, through a narrowly defined examination process known as the 11-plus exam. This system segregates pupils into secondary modern school or grammar school, each with its own particular curriculum, expectations and set of values. In the 1950s and 1960s, selection was the norm and pupils/students who had experi-ence of this segregated education bare the scars even as adults. Writing in the *Times Educational Supplement* (3.5.02), Andrew Granath cites examples of permanent feelings of inferiority and the creation of family rifts caused by pupils being selected at age 11. Adults reporting back on the experience talk about bearing the weight of parental disappointment, being shamed for lack of academic ability, family tensions being caused by one sibling passing the 11-plus and the other failing, and chances of going to university being denied owing to inferior school facilities and low teacher expectations. Alongside this gloomy picture there are, naturally, exceptions: pupils who achieved in spite of discrimination, often citing the support of individ-ual teachers who valued individual difference. Nonetheless, this is an example of values that conspired to devalue individuals and create low expectations of large groups of pupils. We must consider carefully the significant effects on pupils of groupings in classroom organisation, in the light of this experience.

Schools both reflect the values of society and interpret them according to their own local context. In so doing, schools can also provide a forum in which dominant values can be challenged. In recent years schools have increasingly acknowledged the importance of teachers actively listening to their pupils on a variety of issues. Recent research into finding positive alternatives to school exclusion has shown that there is a significant link between teachers and schools who actively listen to their pupils and a decrease in the number of pupils excluded. For example, teachers who enter into a dialogue and who empathise with their pupils 'made a crucial difference to the quality of the students' lives and their commitment to school' (Cooper *et al.* 2002: 188). In terms of whole-school approaches, school councils have been developed to 'promote a practical understanding of democratic procedures and the rights and responsibilities of citizenship.' (Halstead and Taylor 2000: 178). School councils provide pupils with the opportunities for increased understanding of management issues, enhancing problem-solving abilities by taking into account the perspectives of others, and improving behaviour through an increased consideration of the rights of others and commensurate responsibilities. In their summary of research findings, Halstead and Taylor (2000) cite John and Osborn (1992), who suggest that

schools with more participation and freedom of expression had a stronger influence on pupils' values than the traditional school; in the former, pupils were more supportive of race and gender equality but also more sceptical about the democratic operation of government.

Such research indicates that where schools have a more democratic ethos, where teachers listen and genuinely consult with pupils, school councils operate more effectively and have a significant role in the formation of inclusive values.

Circle time is a well-used approach, particularly in Primary schools, and it is growing in Secondary schools, as a means of promoting confidence, self-esteem and social responsibility and cohesion within the class:

Circle time may also help pupils to learn to talk about their feelings, to gain a sense of belonging to a group or community, to develop qualities such as trust, responsibility, empathy, co-operation, caring behaviour and respect for the feelings of others and to engage in personal reflection and clarify their own values. (Halsted and Taylor 2000: 185)

For this method to be effective, it requires teachers to have a clear understanding of the rationale and ways of facilitating the process that empowers the pupils. Not surprisingly, Circle time is most effective if its underlying values are consistent with those of the teacher, the classroom and the school.

Pupils learn a great deal about values from the feedback they receive from their teachers. It is suggested that this may be overt or implicit. The language and jargon used by teachers and experienced by pupils, to describe individuals, will not only impact upon pupils' performance but on their concepts of self-esteem. The labelling of pupils by teachers can lead to self-fulfilling prophecies and negative associations. Teachers must be mindful of the language they use to describe pupils, both publicly in talking with other professionals, parents/carers and in writing reports or assessments, as well as within the confines of the staffroom. The quality of teachers' comments can influence the expectations of pupils, parents/carers and other colleagues.

Do pupils have a sense that their opinions are valued? As reflective teachers, we should allow our thinking to be challenged and changed by feedback from pupils. This will demonstrate the value we put on learning through reflective interaction. Pupils' sense of self is shaped by their experiences, and how they construct understanding through experiences has, in turn, significant implications for teachers. How do schools respond to the social and cultural environment in which their pupils live? As has been discussed earlier, actively listening to what pupils have to say about their experiences of school is one of the most significant values a teacher can model and encourage. Research shows (Cooper *et al.* 2002, Corbett 2001, O'Brien and Guiney 2002, Hargreaves and Fullan 1998) that teachers who view problems as opportunities, who are ready to consider that the feedback they receive from their pupils is information upon which they can act in order to better develop their practice; in short, teachers who listen and learn from their pupils are teachers who value their pupils. This leads us to the second section, which considers teachers' expectations.

Teacher expectations and values

Qualifying to Teach states that teachers must have high expectations of all pupils (TTA 2002a: 2; see also Chapter 1 of this volume). This is echoed within numerous Government documents and guidelines (e.g. DfES (2001) *Special Educational Needs Code of Practice*, the National Curriculum of 2000, and DfEE's *Excellence for All Children* (1997). But what does 'having high expectations' mean or look like in our classrooms? According to the Standards it means that teachers will have an understanding that 'all their pupils are capable of significant progress and that their potential for learning is unlimited' (TTA 2002a: 2). A common theme is that of raising attainment for all through inclusive educational practices.

Inclusive approaches to education require teachers to hold inclusive values. Inclusive values are concerned with education for diversity. Jenny Corbett (2000) suggests that a connective pedagogy is at the heart of inclusive practices. A connective pedagogy addresses individual needs, engages institutional resources and relates to community values. It is, most importantly, about linking individuals into the curriculum so that it has relevance and is meaningful to them. Important aspects of pedagogy will include encouraging pupils to think about how they learn, in order to evaluate their learning (Moore 2000). An important element of this pedagogy is for teachers to develop emotional literacy for themselves and their pupils. Teachers who provide emotional support for their pupils understand the links between feelings and a motivation to learn. It also requires of teachers a readiness to use different styles in their teaching and, most importantly, to take account of cultural factors. However, Moore suggests that whilst teachers cannot have an intimate knowledge of all the cultures of their pupils, 'they can avoid making easy assumptions about those cultures or refusing to acknowledge that they exist at all' (Moore 2000: 114). Are teachers aware of the cultural bias that exists in the Curriculum and how do they incorporate pupils' existing experiences and cultural preferences into lessons? Bourdieu's theory of 'cultural capital' suggests that learners are advantaged or disadvantaged by the value systems they encounter at school. How do teachers acknowledge, respect and value the cultural capital that learners bring to school? Schools and teachers must be sensitive to and value the identities of students and make efforts to reinforce the confidence, motivation and self-esteem of pupils by including in the Curriculum their histories, languages, religions and cultures (Blair *et al.* (1999) cited in Moore 2000).

There is no doubt that pupils are influenced by the quality of relationships which they experience in school. The attitudes, behaviours and values that teachers bring to their classrooms will significantly contribute to a pupils' own sense of developing values. I have already identified the way that the personal beliefs of teachers are reflected in many and subtle ways and how this impacts upon the pupils they teach. If it is the role of teachers to meet the needs of all learners in their classes, then it is incumbent upon teachers to reflect critically 'on their pedagogical repertoire, their assumptions about curriculum and classroom and school organisation, along with the ideologies that inform these components of schooling' (Cole 1997: 64). A teacher's pedagogical approach will influence the learning opportunities offered to pupils. Teachers who value and encourage spirited and enquiring minds will do so in a way that complements and supports a broad and balanced educational experience, which includes diverse cultural and linguistic dimensions. The promotion of attitudes that foster enquiry and investigation rather than the right answer will be an integral part of a culture that promotes intellectual curiosity. So, how do teachers model and promote intellectual curiosity working as they do within a well-defined, some might say, straitjacket of a curriculum? Observations in classrooms reveal that teachers who foster interactive approaches to teaching and learning, where pupils explore, experience and investigate, are better able to maintain that intellectual curiosity characteristic of young children. The principles of an interactive approach according to Collis and Lacey (1996: 13) are:

- Learning is contingent upon good interpersonal relationships.
- There is sensitivity to feedback from the learner.
- Focus is on understanding rather than skill acquisition.
- Emphasis is on respect, negotiation and participation. The pupils' contribution is valued and positively built upon.

Within classrooms this is represented by cooperative group work, the use of talk to co-construct knowledge, pupils making choices and thus having more responsibility for their own learning and pupils' monitoring their own learning. This kind of interactive learning is usually fun and motivating. The use of games is often observed in interactive teaching since they provide opportunities to practise skills in a modelled way, where it is safe to make mistakes.

An important aspect of having high expectations is concerned with the language we use. Language is a powerful medium with great potential. It can, amongst other things, raise self-esteem through the use of specific praise or it can lead to negative, self-fulfilling prophecies, reinforcing stereotypes based on characteristics that are traditionally attached to a label, for example, the stereotype of the child with Down Syndrome as 'happy and loving'. The Index for Inclusion (CSIE 2000) makes a point of not using the label of 'special educational needs' (SEN) unless it is referring to its embodiment in legislation or policy framework. This is because the label, SEN, can lead to lowered expectations and can encourage teachers to think that pupils who are categorised as having SEN are primarily the responsibility of a specialist teacher or school. An approach that focuses on individual difficulties 'has limitations as a way of resolving educational difficulties and can be a barrier to the development of inclusive practices in schools' (CSIE 2000: 13).

As teachers are required to have regard to government guidance, I should like to consider for a moment the influence of political policy on values. It is interesting to notice the contradiction here between the revised *SEN Code of Practice* (DfES 2001) and the *Index for Inclusion* (CSIE 2000), both of which are endorsed by the Government, but which convey very different, and one might suggest, contradictory messages. The former still focuses essentially upon within-child deficits, with its emphasis on individual education plans, while the latter not only embraces the learning of all pupils, but also encourages the consideration of factors beyond the individual pupil to those of the culture, policy and practice of schools. The values implicit within these documents are somewhat different. Teachers are concerned with reducing barriers to learning for a broad range of pupils, including, for example, those from minority ethnic communities, and those disadvantaged for reasons of gender, disability, sexuality and social class (Cole (ed.) 2002; Hill and Cole (eds) 2001). They have a responsibility to cater for the needs of travellers, looked-after children, refugees, children who move schools frequently, pupils for whom English is an additional language, and pupils living in poverty.

Peter Mittler suggests that 'although we use the language of diversity, social justice and equal opportunities, the society in which we live is still riddled with inequalities, which are in turn reflected in the education system' (Mittler 2000: 12, see also Cole (ed.) (2002); Hill and Cole (eds) (2001)). Teachers thus have a significant role to play in shifting the interests of disadvantaged groups, from the margins of society and school to centre stage, in part through a close examination of their own attitudes and beliefs. How a teacher's values chime with local, national and global directions on equality issues, and how far teachers are prepared to enter into a reflective debate at both a conceptual and a real-life classroom level, will determine how successful change might be (Mittler 2000). Research (e.g. Sebba and Sachdev 1997) and personal experience indicates that the greatest barriers to inclusion are the attitudes and values that teachers possess. How hearts and minds are won over will remain to be seen but certainly the use, by schools, of the *Index for Inclusion* (CSIE 2000) is a step in the right direction for a close scrutiny of values in policy, practice and culture.

The National Curriculum, as an ethnocentric curriculum, supports a largely monocultural approach to education, failing as it does to reflect the diversity of culture and community, and it marginalises and excludes large numbers of pupils in multicultural Britain. As a teacher it is of vital importance that we look at the ways the formal curriculum is planned and taught, so that it 'helps children acquire appropriate positive attitudes and values and a healthy self esteem' (Macpherson 2000: 99). While it is not in itself a curriculum, the *Index for Inclusion* does provide us with a rather different view from either the National Curriculum or the *SEN Code of Practice*, and encourages schools to take an approach that celebrates diversity in all forms. It is a tool that can assist schools in 'a detailed examination of the possibilities for increasing learning and participation in all aspects of their school for all students' (CSIE 2000: 7). In attempting to make the curriculum accessible and relevant, teachers will be required to differentiate what they teach and how they teach it, in ways that do not lead to further segregation. (Mittler 2000).

To summarise this section, our values contribute to the kind of teacher we are or hope to be. The things we believe in underpin our professional identity. We teach in certain ways because we have certain beliefs that guide our teaching methods. Reflecting on our practices as teachers may give some insight or indication into what we value and why. It is important, therefore, for teachers to have a thorough understanding of how pupils learn as well as knowledge of the way ethnicity, gender, class, religion, poverty and disability impact upon teaching and learning and educational achievement. 'A key implication of all this is that teachers need to review on a regular basis their beliefs and attitudes about learners and learning and challenge constantly the expectations they have of their pupils, as well as seeking to understand and enhance the motivation of those they are teaching' (Gipps and MacGilchrist 1999: 59). In order to enter into this spirit of reflection, teachers will need the time, support and the inclination to think and discuss with colleagues who may have very different views on values (Ghaye and Ghaye 1998). In this way, teachers will be 'thoughtful, questioning, perceptive as well as skilled – in the pursuit of a democratic, anti-authoritarian, socially responsible, socially just and equal society' (Hill *et al.* 1997: 108).

Economic and political factors

It is almost impossible to separate out the personal development of one's values from wider economic and political influences. As we have seen through the previous two sections, we do not grow up and go to school in a political or cultural vacuum. Our experience of school is inevitably controlled by the economic and political agenda of the day. This is evident from the discussion so far, which has made reference to a number of government policy initiatives that have had a profound impact upon what happens in schools. Such initiatives are in turn affected by global economic processes. For example, Cole (1998; 2002b) has argued that the Blair Government's mantra of 'Education, Education, Education' needs to be seen in the light of New Labour's commitment to global capitalism. In order for Britain to produce a flex-ible workforce – a requirement of contemporary capitalism – it is important for edu-cation to be reformed (for business to have a greater influence both within schools and as the recipient of contracted-out education services). Globalisation is used ideologically as the *raison d'être* of New Labour's education policy, and modernisa-tion (a final break with Old Labour and socialist values) is the conduit through which the policy is introduced (ibid.; see also Allen *et al.* 1999). As I have suggested above, however, education does not only reflect economic and political processes, it can also challenge them. An understanding of this dynamic will certainly be part of any discussion that is related to values, including a consideration of the conse-quences of policy on teaching and learning. It is clear that there are negative effects of government policy on how schools and teachers take on board the concept of inclusion as an equal rights issue. Legislation and guidance has seen the emphasis on standards and league tables, and competition that exerts exclusionary forces for example, whilst at the same time stressing the inclusion of pupils with complex learning and emotional needs.

Legislation and the value systems enshrined therein have always heavily influenced education. Currently there appears to be, at best, a somewhat fragmented and contra-dictory number of government policies contributing to an education system where there are conflicts of values and thus incompatible demands. Booth (2000) refers to this as a disconnection of educational policy from their social effects. We are now living in an enterprise culture, driven by the market forces of competition, consumer choice, targets, league tables, a national system of normative assessment with the results used to measure school effectiveness and a tenuous encouragement of inclu-sive education. What is the potential impact of consumer-type policy upon teacher and pupil values? To return to a view expressed earlier in this chapter, it is incumbent upon teachers to scrutinise their values and practices to analyse and reflect on eco-nomic and political realities and to enable and encourage their pupils to do likewise in order to promote equality, to challenge stereotyping and to counter discrimination.

In conclusion

It is not possible to discuss professional values without being clear about our own values. Changes imposed by government legislation impact upon the culture and values of the schools we work in. In this situation, how can a teacher shape what kind of teacher they are or aspire to be and what goes on in their classrooms? Susan Hart reminds us that, 'while the pressures of classroom teaching clearly impose major constraints on what is possible, the extent to which teaching is reflective is also a function of teachers' values and aspirations for children's learning and the extent to which classroom practices have been developed and adjusted reflect these' (Hart 2000: 41).

Whatever their background, teachers have to respond to the diverse values of the pupils, parents/carers and community they work with. Teachers must also support their pupils so that they appreciate that differences between and among people are usual, and at the same time develop the skills necessary to cope with any conflicts this might create.

Teachers will need to have opportunities to discuss values, to reflect on their own values and scrutinise their practices in honest and transparent ways. This is a challenging task, but in this way we might ensure a community in which everyone is valued, in order to secure the highest social, emotional and academic achievements of all pupils.

Note

1. While pupils need to understand that values are relative, they also need to consider the possibility of a core of absolute values – social justice being one.

References

Allen, M., Benn, C., Chitty, C. *et al.* (1999) *Business, Business, Business: New Labour's Education Policy.* London: Tufnell Press.

Blair, M. and Bourne, J., with Coffin, C., Creese, A. and Kenner, C. (1999) *Making the Difference: Teaching and Learning Strategies in Successful Multi-Ethnic Schools.* DfEE Research Briefs, Research No. 59. London: Department for Education and Employment.

Booth, T. (2000) 'Inclusion and Exclusion Policy in England: Who Controls the Agenda?', in F. Armstrong, D. Armstrong and L. Barton (eds) *Inclusive Education.* London: David Fulton Publishers.

Cairns, J. (2000) 'Schools, Community and the Developing Values of Young Adults: Towards an Ecology of Education in Values', in J. Cairns, R. Gardner and D. Lawton (eds) (2000) *Values and the Curriculum.* London: Woburn Press.

Centre for Studies on Inclusive Education (CSIE) (2000) *Index for Inclusion.* SIE in collaboration with Centre for Educational Needs, University of Manchester; Centre for Education Research, Canterbury Christ Church College.

Cole, M. (1997) 'Equality and Primary Education: What Are the Conceptual Issues?' in M. Cole, D. Hill and S. Shan (eds) *Promoting Equality in Primary Schools.* London: Cassell.

Cole, M. (1998) 'Globalization, modernization and competitiveness: a critique of the New Labour Project in education', *International Studies in Sociology of Education,* 8(3), 315–32.

Cole, M. (ed.) (2002) *Education, Equality and Human Rights.* London: Routledge/Falmer.

Cole, M. (2002) 'New Labour, globalization and social justice: the role of education', in P. McLaren, H. Sunker and G. Fischman (eds) *Critical Theories, Radical Pedagogies and Global Conflicts.* Lanham, Maryland: Rowman & Littlefield.

Collis, M. and Lacey, P. (1996) *Interactive Approaches to Teaching*. London: David Fulton Publishers.

Cooper, P. Drummond, M. J., Hart, S., Lovey, J. and McLaughlin, C. (2002) *Positive Alternatives to Exclusion*. London: Routledge/Falmer.

Corbett, J. (2001) *Supporting Inclusive Education*. London: Routledge/Falmer

DfEE (1997) *Excellence for All Children*. London: The Stationery Office.

DfES (2001) *Special Educational Needs Code of Practice*. London: DfES.

DfES/QCA (2001) *Planning, Teaching and Assessing the Curriculum for Pupils with Learning Difficulties*. London: DfES.

Ghaye, A. and Ghaye, K. (1998) *Teaching and Learning through Critical Reflective Practice*. London: David Fulton Publishers.

Gipps, C. and MacGilchrist, B. (1999) 'Primary School Learners' in Mortimore, P. (ed.) *Understanding Pedagogy and its Impact on Learning*. London: Paul Chapman.

Granath, A. (2002) *Times Educational Supplement*, 'Talkback', 3.5.02. 'Rift at 11-plus Still Smarts After 40 Years'.

Halstead, J. M. and Taylor, M. J. (eds) (1996) *Values in Education and Education in Values*. London: Falmer Press.

Halstead, J. M. and Taylor, M. J. (2000) 'Learning and Teaching about Values: a Review of Recent Research'. *Cambridge Journal of Education*, 3(2), 169–202.

Hargreaves, A. and Fullan, M. (1998) *What's Worth Fighting For In Education?* Buckingham: Open University Press.

Hart, S. (2000) *Thinking through Teaching: A Framework for Enhancing Participation and Learning*. London: David Fulton Publishers.

Haydon, G. (1997) *Teaching about Values: A New Approach*. London: Cassell.

Hill, D. and Cole, M. (eds) (2001) *Schooling and Equality*. London: Kogan Page.

Hill, D., Cole, M. and Williams, C. (1997) 'Equality and Primary Teacher Education' in M. Cole, D. Hill and S. Shan (eds) *Promoting Equality in Primary Schools*. London: Cassell.

John, P. D. and Osborn, A. (1992) 'The influence of school ethos on pupils' citizenship attitudes', *Educational Review*, 44, 153–65.

MacBeath, J. and Mortimore, P. (2001) 'School Effectiveness and Improvement: the Story So Far' in J. MacBeath and P. Mortimore (eds) *Improving School Effectiveness*. Buckingham: Open University Press.

Macpherson, P. (2000) 'Creating a Positive Classroom Climate' in K. Jacques and R. Hyland (eds) *Professional Studies*. Learning Matters Ltd.

Mittler, P. (2000) *Working Towards Inclusive Education*. London: David Fulton Publishers.

Moore, A. (2000) *Teaching and Learning: Pedagogy, Curriculum and Culture*. London: Routledge/Falmer.

O'Brien, T. (2001) in P. Benton and T. O'Brien (eds) *Special Needs and The Beginning Teacher*. London: Continuum.

O'Brien, T. and Guiney, D. (2001) *Differentiation in Teaching and Learning*. London: Continuum.

QCA (2000) *Curriculum 2000.* Appendix on General Inclusion Statement. London: QCA.

Sebba, J. and Sachdev, D. (1997) *What Works in Inclusive Education.* Ilford, Essex: Barnardo's.

Taylor, Monica J. (1996) 'Voicing their Values: Pupils' Moral and Cultural Experience', in J. Mark Halstead and Monica J. Taylor (eds) *Values in Education and Education in Values.* London: Falmer Press.

Teacher Training Agency (TTA) (2002a) *Qualifying to Teach: Professional Standards for Qualified Teacher Status and Requirements for Initial Teacher Training.* London: DfES.

Teaching Training Agency (TTA) (2002b) *Handbook on Guidance on QTS Standards and ITT Requirements.* London: DfES.

CHAPTER 4

The challenge of parental involvement

Linda Hurley

Introduction

In Section 1.4 of the Teacher Training Agency's *Qualifying to Teach* (TTA 2002: 6) it is stated that those awarded QTS must demonstrate that they 'can communicate sensitively and effectively with parents and carers, recognising their roles in pupils' learning, and their rights, responsibilities and interests in this.'

Parental[1] support for schools is widely recognised as a crucial determinant of educational performance. Since the Plowden Report of 1967 (DES 1967), which highlighted the importance of schools and parents working together, the relationship between the two is regularly pulled back into focus (Bastiani 1989; Epstein 1995; Sammons *et al.* 1995) etc. However, despite universal recommendations for schools and parents to work together, implementation of this as a practice is patchy and not without its challenges. There has been advice for schools on how to engage parents but they are often seen as a homogenous group, devoid of class, culture, sexuality and diversity, and whose willingness to engage in their children's education is whimsical. Recently, however, research has investigated the nature of parent response and the factors affecting it. (Tizard *et al.* 1981; Lareau 1989, Brown 1993; Pollard and Filer 1996; Vincent 1996; Reay 1999; Hughes and Macnaughton 2000). This chapter is an attempt to identify these factors and the challenges they present to teachers with a view to addressing the needs of schools and *all* parents. It draws on the work of Epstein (1995) and research cited above, and sets parental involvement against the backdrop of the recent government initiative of inclusion. It also includes data from my own research on parental involvement in areas of social exclusion.

The principle of inclusion

In 2000, the Centre for Studies on Inclusive Education published an *Index for Inclusion*, a document giving guidance to schools and promoting the Government's agenda on providing inclusive education for all children.

The *Index* challenges schools to reflect the communities they serve, to celebrate differences, and become places where 'diversity is not seen as a problem to be overcome but a rich resource to support the learning of all' (Centre for Studies on Inclusive Education 2000: 12). It includes a recognition that parents and families are members of communities which have a right and a responsibility to be included in the education of children, that they have valuable contributions to make and are an essential part of the community of the school. It takes for granted that a truly inclusive school welcomes all parents and regards them as 'partners' in a child's education.

Parents as partners

The document 'Effective Schools and Home–School Partnership Roles: a Framework for Parental Involvement' provides a model for parents as 'co-communicators, co-supporters, co-learners and co-decision makers' (Chrispeels 1996). In school policy documents, of which there are many, parents are often referred to as 'partners'. However, even in schools where they are involved, some parents are highly active whilst others are rarely seen. Why is this? What makes communication with some so easy whilst with others it is laboured and misunderstood? Perhaps the answer to that question lies in diversity. In some playgrounds parents might be mistaken for teachers whilst in others that is unlikely. Does a true partnership between them depend on similarities in class, culture, sexuality and gender? How likely is a 'legitimate discourse' (Habermas 1973) where there is little common ground? Relationships between lay-people and professionals are always imbalanced in terms of knowledge and can, therefore, be power relationships. (Merttens *et al.* 1996; Vincent 1996; Reay 1999). How do teachers, as professionals, deal with these relationships, share knowledge and therefore empower parents to share in the educational experience of their children?

Those who are involved in their children's schooling tend to be those whose cultural framework echoes that of the school, who agree and comply with its practices and do not question its philosophy, that is, middle-class, white heterosexual families. Children from these families continue to benefit from improvements in the educational system while, on the other hand, 'the link between low attainment and disadvantage remains strong and persistent' (OFSTED 1999: 24).

In recent years, schools have recognised a responsibility to meet the needs of an increasingly multicultural society and begun to address this by introducing multicultural literature and recognising a variety of faiths and practices. This is a start towards a dialogue between home and school for those from minority ethnic communities. However, ethnicity is not the only reason for parental exclusion. Whilst most teachers are white and middle class, and in primary schools are women, many parent and carers are not. Social class is a factor largely unrecognised by teachers as being responsible for parents' exclusion from their children's schools.[2] The overwhelming reason for this is not a lack of interest or commitment, but:

- Their own experience at school, which was one of alienation leading to poor attendance and leading to . . .
- Lack of skills and knowledge, leading to . . .
- Low self-esteem and fear of school, sometimes compounded by teachers' lack of awareness of the significance of the above (Hurley 2000a).

Reay notes that although working-class parents are anxious to support their children's education, this support is characterised by 'lack of knowledge, of inappropriate educational standards and an uncertainty about their competence as educators' (Reay 1999: 78).

In fact, however confident and successful parents are as members of their community, this success is often not transferrable to school. These findings reaffirm the critical importance of the teacher/parent relationship. They are issues which we, as teachers, committed to the notion of inclusion, need to consider by examining our own perceptions and attitudes and the ethos of our schools.

What follows is an analysis of the different types of parental involvement as defined by Epstein (1995), the challenges they pose to us as professionals, and some practical suggestions for meeting these challenges. All teacher and parent quotes are from recent research (Hurley 2000a; Hurley 2000b)[3] unless otherwise stated.

Six types of ways to involve parent/carers in schools

Epstein (1995) identified six types of parental involvement. These are:

1. Parenting;
2. Communicating;
3. Volunteering;
4. Learning at home;
5. Decision-making;
6. Collaborating with the community.

These six types are followed by an explanation of the school's role.

1. Parenting – to help all parent/carers establish home environments to support children as students

It is widely recognised by schools that parenting skills have a significant impact on a child's development and progress at school. In most cases parents feel their role is paramount and demonstrate an impressive list of skills which reflect devotion to their children:

'The kids are my job.' – Bunty, a Mum.

Jane, a learning support teacher helping children and parents with their literacy skills, was working with Carol and her daughter. Carol had been banned from school premises for aggressive behaviour but always turned up for the literacy session, which took place in an annexe:

> *'Carol came every single week, even though she'd just been banned from the school. She always had her folder with her games in it, brought all the books back.'* – Jane, learning support teacher.

Research also has shown conclusively that *all* parents are interested in their child's education (Tizard *et al.* 1981; Lareau 1989; Reay 1999). However, some schools have their own ideas about what makes a 'good' parent:

> *'The home I went in was clean, very organised, but there were no books . . . which was quite shocking because it was one of the better homes and I did expect to see things around.'* – Susan, teacher.

> *'She's worn those clothes every day for two years. Goodness knows when she washes them.'* – Catherine, teacher.

These comments summarise a school's notion of a deficit in some homes. Susan had been '*shocked*' because of a predetermined idea of what she would see in a '*better home*'. She recognised cleanliness and order and how these might be significant in a child's application to school, but she didn't see books. Books are an obvious link between home and school. They represent 'cultural resources' (Baker *et al.* 2001) common to both contexts, and children who come from literate families where books are part of their lives will bring that experience to school. Different cultural practices and financial priorities are embedded in homes and their material resources and do not necessarily replicate the classroom. There are also many styles of parenting, linked with social class, financial resources and culture. Both quotes fail to make the connection between poverty and resources. The comments above are those of teachers who see themselves as one of the 'natural guardians of democracy' (Walkerdine and Lucey 1989: 40) commenting on what they see as 'inappropriate' parenting skills. It is about teachers having fixed ideas about what homes should look like, based on their own homes, and what parents should do, but has nothing to do with partnership or 'co-communication'.

Home-visiting is common practice for early years teachers. It is an opportunity to share information about culture, background, children's talents and needs, and the challenge for teachers must be to listen as well as lead. It is an opportunity for teachers to learn of different cultural attitudes to education and schools, for example, different cultural practices in learning, and acquire vital information about religious beliefs, which languages are spoken at home and any special dietary needs. Some parents may be bemused by western educational informality and teaching methods like the use of play, particularly when their own experience of schooling was formal. It is also the case that some parents feel vulnerable with a professional visiting their home. These parents need to know that no value judgements are being made and that teachers visiting are genuinely interested in what they have to say about their children and in them as people. This requires a disposition which accepts diverse lifestyles without making judgements, and a sensitivity which reflects that disposition. What needs to be communicated is a desire to help schools understand families and families to understand schools.

Some schools advise parents on providing a home environment supportive to school. They run meetings about school issues to inform families and provide a forum for debate. Where these are successful the school will respond to parents' requests for topics of information which might begin as queries about practical issues like school lunches, but have the potential to develop into more pertinent issues dealing with real concerns like children's behaviour. Many people take advantage of these sessions and find them an effective way of forming relationships with others.

However, the challenge for schools is how to involve *all* parents, therefore the agenda must be something they find relevant and important. Any leaflets produced should be clear and available in other languages, and for parents with poor literacy skills, supported by word of mouth. One idea to try might be to use simple posters, perhaps because these are likely to be more striking than a paragraph in a newsletter. In addition, terminology is important – 'workshop' sounds more interesting and interactive than 'meeting' and might be less prohibitive to parents who are more comfortable with an informal setting. Some schools have found it useful to draw on friendly and established parents who might look out for those who need support, particularly if those parents can act as interpreters. Parents often have babysitting problems, and meetings are often attended by only one partner. Whilst crèche provision is useful for some, it is essential to others and a selection of rotated times including evenings might enable both partners to attend. It might also be useful to remember that meetings do not have to be held at school, and some schools take advantage of community facilities such as Health Centres, Family Centres, Community Centres and churches. Finally, teachers should recognise that not everyone belongs in a conventional family setting. For those who are disabled, access must be considered and a home visit considered if this is not possible. The message here is flexibility. For parents whose own school experience was less than satisfactory, these initial meetings will set the scene for future involvement and mutual support.

2. Communicating – to design effective forms of school-to-home and home-to-school communications about school programmes and children's progress

Schools are obliged to inform parents of school policies and procedures. Communication can be written, as in the school prospectus, newsletters and end-of-term reports, or can be verbal, as in curriculum meetings or meetings between parents and teachers on Open Evening.

Teachers are, evidently, communicators. They share expertise and experience with one another and with other professionals from other agencies. They share vital information about their policies and about individual children. We accept that good teachers share messages.

Parents are statutorily entitled to information about their children's progress according to national assessment tests and also according to teacher assessments. Teachers regularly report to them on pupils' attainment and progress orally in face-to-face meetings and in writing. Written reports give information about National Curriculum levels with reference to level descriptors, and for younger children make reference to the Early Learning Goals and appropriate 'stepping stones' leading to them. Needless to say, if reports are to mean anything at all, parents will have an awareness of children's targets, how progress has been achieved, of assessment procedures, and how their child compares with other children of the same age. If children have special educational needs, parents will need to be informed of those needs, what the school is doing and how they themselves can give support. Parents, legally, must be regularly consulted about a child's Individual Education Plan (IEP) and be given enough information to be able to support learning at home (e.g. *exactly* what strategy is the school using to improve the child's playground behaviour? Can this process be continued at home and how?). Written information must be clear, concise and readable but always be based on what the child *can* do as well as what she/he is working towards. In this way, parents are enabled to be 'co-communicators, co-supporters, co-learners and co-decision-makers'. But establishing this will depend on a real dialogue between home and school. Parents need to know about how schools work but to be effective, schools and teachers need to listen to parents. What do children like to do when they are at home? Is there anything happening at home which might have an effect on behaviour and learning? The school ethos will influence the success of this.

'At my last school parents had access to school quite freely. If wet, parents would come in and wait – here they are kept outside . . . I don't think it helps.' – Pat, teacher.

'The school has an "open door" policy. If I'm worried I can just pop in.' – Alice, parent.

The quotes above are about two very different schools. In one, parents were kept outside even in the rain, whilst in the other they could 'pop in' when there was a concern. It is obvious in which school home–school relationships were more successful. Parents who are less confident about their role in their children's education are quite likely to think that what they have to say isn't important enough to warrant teacher time, and the same parents can be reluctant to make appointments to see a teacher (Reay 1999), but may grab an opportunity to relate significant information. Vital information can be shared at any time, particularly incidentally, like first thing in the morning. In the same way, valuable information about learning should be communicated not only in end-of-term reports but also in memos, reading diaries and behaviour logs and can provide a regular, sometimes daily dialogue between home and school.

Communication with parents always has the potential to be challenging and will depend on sensitivity and tact whilst delivering clear messages. For any people whose children are having problems at school it is a worrying time. It is for this reason that teachers need to understand parents' perceptions in order not to make assumptions, generalisations and stereotypical judgements. So listening is important.

Challenges for schools might be to review the readability of notices from school. Are they also produced with non-English readers in mind? Are they clear and simple and are teachers aware of parents whose literacy skills are poor? Is there support for these parents in the form of informal and verbal information? Is communication two-way? If other agencies such as the Educational Welfare Officer or the Speech Therapist are involved, whose responsibility is it to make sure everyone is informed regularly? Are there enough opportunities for unplanned meetings between teachers and parents, and do they feel able to come into school at any time to voice a concern? Some messages teachers have to give are tough but are better informed and easier to deliver if there have been regular opportunities for an honest dialogue.

3. Volunteering – to recruit parent/carer help and support

Increasingly, teachers depend on voluntary help from parents. Classroom helpers are a common feature of primary schools and many teachers would say they could not meet the demands of the children and the curriculum without them. Parents are often seen in school offices helping with administration, and seasonally, staff-rooms are taken over by groups of parents making decorations and counting money. These parents are 'co-supporters'. In some schools they are easy to find but in others they are hard to come by. It is often the schools in affluent areas where parents are most commonly seen, where even though parents lead hectic lives, sometimes juggling work and family, they have access to more resources (like a car) and are therefore able to fit classroom sessions into busy schedules. These parents recognise the importance of a child's success at school. They know their own education gave them opportunities and are determined that their own children should have the same advantages. In other less affluent areas, parents can be elusive. Though adults are more likely to be unemployed and therefore may have more time, helping in their child's classroom is the last thing they would choose to do. Requests from school for help are often ignored and schools are left with the false impression that parent/carers don't care about their children's education.

'I listen to the children read, sharpen pencils. I didn't care what I did.' – Anna, parent.

'I come in to help sort out the library and that kind of stuff, not actually doing anything with the children . . . it's just that with reading, if there's a word they don't know and I don't know it, that's when I'm going to have trouble.' – Alice, parent.

The parent quotes above are from parents with very different experiences. Anna is a confident woman with professional qualifications who took time out from her job in a bank to bring up her children. She has just gone back to work part-time but goes into her children's school regularly. She is so confident in school that she could almost be mistaken for one of the teachers, and will *'do anything'*. In fact, she sees it as part of her role as a mother to find out what is going on at school *'to make sure that what we're doing at home doesn't contradict what they're doing at school'*. (Anna, parent.) However, for Alice, volunteering to help in the classroom is a different matter. Alice's reading skills are poor. Alice could not be mistaken for one of the teachers and her body language shows she does not feel at home. She frequently worries that someone will ask her to do something she can't manage and understands why some parents are reluctant to get involved:

> *'I manage to come to school and not be frightened but I've heard lots of people say because of what happened to them at school when they were children, they've found it difficult to get involved in stuff at their children's school.'* – Alice, parent.

In the same school another parent had been approached personally by a teacher looking for a volunteer. On arrival, she said:

> *'I've been dreading this all day.'* – Chloe, parent.

To teachers this might seem strange, but for some parents, fear of school is very real.

We know that some parent/carers are more in tune with schools than others. They 'fit in' more easily, they know what to do more or less without being told. They will *'do anything'*. We are also aware that there are significant benefits for children and parent/carers as well as schools when they are included. Involvement in the classroom can give knowledge about what's being taught and how, which clearly benefits the child, but parents and children who are part of the school also acquire 'institutional habitus' (Reay 1999), a sense of belonging which demystifies what might otherwise be an unfamiliar environment. Habitus is knowledge and acceptance of 'the way things are', the 'social game embodied and turned into second nature' (Bourdieu 1991: 63). Research has shown that children with institutional habitus are more likely to succeed at school than those without (Pollard and Filer 1996; Reay 1999; Hurley 2000b). Alice had poor literacy skills, so was nervous about helping in the classroom, but her Mum had been the caretaker in her primary school and with her institutional habitus she had the confidence to get involved. She helped in the library, she made cakes for the school fair and she broke up tiles for the mosaic artist during Art Week. Both of Alice's children were doing well at school and the teachers valued Alice's support.

Even confident parents can be reticent about coming in to help. They are often aware of the dynamics between the professional and the lay-person and feel unsure of their competence. For these parents some schools provide training and find work which will reflect their interests. In Alice's school parents regularly make props for school plays. For a recent pantomime the costumes looked as though they had been made by professionals. Another group of parents is currently making 'Story Sacks' to go with books they have chosen from the local bookshop. These parents feel valued.

Challenges for schools are how to involve *all* parents. Teachers will not know of interests and skills unless they listen and ask, which means setting time for a dialogue with parents and giving the message that all skills are valued – particularly those which will give the children experience of culture and diversity. Some parents are puzzled by requests by schools for volunteers. They expect school matters to be handled by teachers. For some families from minority ethnic communities, participation in children's education may be an unfamiliar experience and the informal atmosphere of the primary classroom very different from their own experience. Opportunity for classroom observation, along with parent–teacher dialogue, will help dispel misunderstandings and give insight into teachers' aims and methods.

Very often, classroom intervention is left to the discretion of individual teachers. These teachers should consider excluded parents. It is easy for teachers to give reasons why certain parents are *'of little use'* (teacher quote, Hurley 2000a) in the classroom but these are the parents who, along with their children, will benefit the most.

Men are rarely seen in some primary schools, which are mainly run by women, but can give credence to activities normally seen to be undertaken by women, like sewing and reading, and all adults can validate non-academic skills which might reflect the interests of the community, like food, growing things, music and sport. Both male and female parents need to know that their skills are recognised and valued even if they did not 'do well' at school themselves and teachers need to remember that schools do not have the monopoly on learning. Parents will teach their children a variety of important skills which, with a little imagination, can be incorporated into the curriculum and make vital links with education at home and in the community.

Schedules for volunteers need to be flexible. Working parents might be able to 'pop in' on an *ad hoc* basis rather than make a regular commitment, or come regularly for half an hour in the morning. Those who are less confident may find it prohibitive to have to sign up on a regular basis but will respond to individual requests for giving up a short time the following day. Some teachers have found that parents will sign up on a blank weekly timetable every Monday morning to commit themselves that week, or that they are willing to come with a friend. Other teachers will welcome parents with toddlers (having done this myself, it is not for the fainthearted but the benefits outweighed the drawbacks).

And finally, schools need to be welcoming places where parents feel valued and included. Experience of diversity in the classroom can only extend learning for children and adults alike.

4. Learning at home – provide information to parent/carers about how to help students at home with homework and other curriculum-related activities, decisions and planning

Schools often have a homework policy explaining to parents how often homework is set and how it should be monitored, but knowledge of the current curriculum and how it is taught in school today is, at best, out of date for non-teachers who are not aware of recent significant educational changes. To counteract this, schools give information explaining current initiatives like national strategies, and hold meetings and workshops for new parents on how they teach core subjects and how parents can help. There have also been innovative projects like the IMPACT maths project encouraging parents to become involved in their children's learning. Schools tend to believe that parents will usually be able to support learning at home but McNamara notes that 'even parents who have excellent contact with school still know little of what their children learn or how to help them' (McNamara *et al.* 2000). For parents whose own experience of school was less than satisfactory, we are asking the impossible:

> *'It's changed a lot since I went to school. It's like with maths – times and long division, no worries. But then you go on to areas. I never really understood that myself. I say "Tell your teacher your Mum can't even do this".'* – Chelsea, parent.

Chelsea's comment shows a recognition of educational changes and a feeling of inadequacy with her own level of curricular knowledge, but, as a parent, the school's expectation is that she will support her child's learning. This places her in the position of a teacher, for which she is ill-equipped, it compounds her feelings of inferiority and confirms her idea of the school as an academic institution in which she has no place. In most of the literature on home involvement there is an omission of how expectations of schools affect the work of parents (Reay 1999). In my own research, homework was one of the areas which caused parents most concern. Those who are least equipped to deal with homework are those from cultures where their school experience has been very different, and those whose own school experiences and attendance were poor. It is also those who live in poor housing:

> *'Brian's a bit more au fait with computers and stuff so he'll help set up the computer if they need it . . . I had to make a mask the other day . . . so he helped him do that."* – Bella, parent.

Bella's comment shows how both she and her partner have developed a *modus vivendi* for homework support. Bella and Brian live in a two-bedroom flat with their four children. They have had to become highly organised and have developed a homework routine which involves finding a quiet space, providing a computer and rotating their time so all the children get attention and someone can look after the toddler. It is sometimes for reasons like these that homework can present a problem to families.

Challenges for schools are, therefore, complex. If parents are to support learning effectively they need to know about the curriculum, teaching methods used and targets for their children which means closer communication with schools. If they are to be 'co-supporters, co-communicators and co-learners' they need information which can be given through workshops, meetings or by observing in schools. This can also be conveyed through the pupils and students themselves, where they are encouraged to discuss at home the important things they are learning. Here, a homework journal can provide a dialogue between home and school with the basis for family and pupil/student participation and the setting of goals.

Homework clubs where there is a teacher to give support work well for some schools. Could the nature of homework also be reviewed? What is homework supposed to do and how? If children are not motivated and parents feel de-skilled, what can schools do? Homework activities do not have to be set, written or recorded but can be based on a family discussion or a game, with children feeding back orally at school the following day. It can also be activity-based, shared with others and linking schoolwork to real life. Schools need to see 'helping at home' as not just about teaching school subjects but about *encouraging, listening, reacting, praising, guiding, monitoring, and discussing*' (Epstein 1995).

5. Decision-making – Include parent/carers in school decisions, developing parent/carer leaders and representatives

'Parental involvement is a good idea as long as parents are vetted.' – Rita, teacher.

If parents are true partners they will be involved in school decision-making. However, teachers rarely see this as part of their role.

The process of making decisions in schools operates at two levels. For practical day-to-day matters the head teacher will make decisions, probably in consultation with the staff and perhaps taking into account views of parents. Decisions regarding policy changes or their implementation will be made by the Governing body of the school which will include parent/carer representation. However, the opportunity for willing parents to be members of a Governing body are necessarily limited by numbers, and those likely to be accepted as 'suitable' representatives both by the school and by other parents are likely to be those whose own lives reflect the institution. This will exclude many working-class parents in general and members of minority ethnic communities, where there is likely to be a discrepancy between the cultural framework of their own lives and that of the school. In addition, opportunities for parents to meet and discuss important issues are limited. There is no forum for them like the staffroom for teachers, and minority voices can easily be lost.

Schools may have an active Parent–Teacher Association or the equivalent, supporting practical activities like fund-raising. But even where parents are actively involved, their role is seen by the school as supportive with no room for criticism. Whether parents have a voice in any decision-making process will depend on the willingness of the school to give them such an opportunity.

The Parents' Charter (DfES 1991), updated in 1994, claims to have made an attempt to accommodate the opinions of parent/carers in the running of their children's schools, but, as previously noted, not all are included. It is white, middle-class, heterosexual parent/carers who remain those most likely to take advantage of the avenues cited above. Although there are, theoretically, opportunities for all parents to participate collectively, the likelihood of this is remote, resulting in a lack of diversity in those having an active voice. Social class, culture, sexuality, gender and disability are all important factors in determining opportunities and willingness to participate.

Initiatives set up by schools to involve more families are 'primarily designed to legitimate the more general action of the institution concerned. Thus they may result in bringing a few, previously excluded individuals into the decision-making process but do little to affect the position of excluded groups' (Vincent 1996). Therefore, parent groups tend to validate established practices rather than challenge them. Only too often, head teachers manage the process so parents who might be trusted with an opportunity to be included are those, from the quote of the teacher above, *vetted by the school*. This is how some remain excluded.

Some parents have always 'got on' with schools better than others and some work hard to cooperate with their children's teachers. Where these relationships work, families and teachers are mutually supportive, but for others, conflict will make an honest dialogue difficult. Their 'assertiveness, aggression or timidity' (Reay 1999) often a result of marginalisation by society, promotes a feeling of inadequacy and is reinforced inadvertently by relationships with teachers (Hurley 2000b). Nevertheless, the individual parent–teacher relationship remains the primary mechanism through which parents can gain access to the workings of the school and the opportunity for parents to be 'co-decision-makers' is remote.

A challenge to schools would be to encourage active discussion amongst parents and to provide a forum for this to happen, perhaps in the form of regular workshops. Where families feel excluded by the nature of their own lives the school can publicly recognise and embrace this diversity. These schools can be proactive in creating an environment where parents can see diversity is celebrated and respected. Parents who have had very different experiences of education will need a more detailed explanation of the way the school works and the philosophies behind it. Parents on the Governing body should be representative of all ethnic and socio-economic groups and members of the Governing body should be given training to demystify the processes of making decisions. Schools should also be prepared to consider that parents have a right to be part of the decision-making process in schools, and to consider the possibility of challenge and change. The Plowden Report (DES 1967) embodied a consensus of home–school relationships which included those parents who were cooperative and supportive. Now schools should consider those who are not and ask themselves why and what they can do about it. Sharing decision-making is not the handing over of power as a quantifiable property where the giver is the loser, but a democratic process where goals are explored and achieved.

6. Collaborating with the community – identify and integrate resources and services from the community to strengthen school programmes, family practices, and student learning and development

> *Whilst complaining that minority group parents do not come to the school, very few teachers visit them at home, spend time in the neighbourhood, for instance in local shops and cafes, or visit the temples, churches or social centres which play an important part in the lives of the families.* (Tizard et al. (1981: 224))

The word 'community' has recently figured large in government attempts to promote a regeneration of moral responsibility. Concepts of 'community care' and, more generally, 'community spirit' have positive associations of shared values and lifestyle whilst assuming a homogenity which supersedes diverse groups (Vincent 1996). However, present-day communities are increasingly heterogeneous in terms of ethnicity, religion, sexuality and social class, and it could be argued that to ignore differences suppresses an opportunity for learning and understanding.

Schools serve communities, and links are essential if children are to be valuable community members, and in this way a community can validate what a school does.

There are many examples of practices currently existing in schools which link schools and communities. These include schools which give information about cultural, recreational, health and social support information for parent/carers and students, maintain links with churches and other religious centres, have links with the local newspaper, participate in recycling schemes, perform drama productions in centres for the elderly and local hospitals, link with local businesses for work experience or school visits, and maintain links with feeder nurseries. Schools provide literacy schemes for adult learners, weekend workshops for family learning to develop, for example, computer skills and community reading projects where retired community members come into school to support children with reading. These schemes support the school whilst at the same time developing the skills of the adults taking part. However, those volunteering will be those with the time, motivation and inclination to be involved in a school-based project.

The challenge to schools might be how to involve more members of the community who might not see themselves as participants in such schemes or as learners. Places on adult literacy schemes are generally taken up by those adults who want to improve their existing skills to enhance their employability rather than those who are semi-literate or have few literacy skills at all (Finlay 1999). Parents who are embarrassed about their skills may be reluctant to volunteer for an opportunity to publicise this special need and may reject opportunities to revisit an experience which has previously resulted in failure and humiliation (Hurley 2000b). However, learning is not confined to school. It is about the broadening of experiences and enjoyment. In one school, parent/carers accompanied their children to an opera. Chelsea, although living a short distance away from the theatre, had never been:

> 'I went to G . . . with them last week. It was brilliant . . . It did open my eyes to the other side, sort of thing, to music.' – Chelsea, parent.

Social class and culture, not to mention financial resources, affect exposure to community and cultural experiences. Schools are in an ideal position to provide experiences for children and include families and carers in those experiences. Good community links will be drawn in schools where 'classroom and extra-curricular activities encourage the participation of all students and draw on their knowledge and experience outside school', where 'Staff mobilise resources within the school and local communities to sustain active learning for all' (Centre for Studies on Inclusive Education 2000: 45).

For parents from minority ethnic communities, there may be a suspicion of school bred by fears of racism. Here, teachers may have to work hard to become more than just an official figure with no profile in the community. Home-visiting alongside an interpreter, and spending time in the community may be a way of teachers acquiring essential information about families and their lives in order to be proactive in creating an environment where racism is unacceptable. It will provide teachers with important, basic information about languages, religions, customs and any possible manifestations of racism, and the acquisition of that information will enhance the status of the teacher.

Conclusion

Relationships between teachers and parent/carers are not just between members of a community and an institution, but between individuals. However, 'interpersonal relations are never, except in appearance, individual to individual relations . . . the truth of the interaction is never entirely contained in the interaction' (Reay 1995). Teachers are agents of the school and their relationships are 'constrained by the hegemony embedded, not just within the practices and understandings of institutions but also within a whole range of social relations and regularities' (Vincent 1996: 6). Thus teachers behave as 'teachers' and think as 'teachers', and their interaction with parents reproduces the social phenomenon which exists outside the individual. It is the way teachers are; not consciously, but because of an unequivocal understanding of their position within the institutional structure which insists on their place in the social structure.

These restraints result in power differentials where, only too often, it is teachers who have the power and parents the anxiety (Bernstein 1990). However, to blame teachers for a lack of participation when that responsibility has always been laid firmly at the feet of parents themselves, would be to replace one fiction with another (Reay 1999).

The vague, consensual terms of 'partnership', 'involvement' and 'dialogue' obscure uncertainties in interpretation and, whilst consistent with parent/carers as 'co-supporters', do little to address *all* parents in their roles as 'co-communicators', 'co-learners' and 'co-decision-makers'. Today, schools have passive parents. The question is – do they want active ones?

Notes

1. Any reference to 'parents' refers to other carers and guardians as well as parents. It is simply for the reasons of literary style that the term 'parents and other carers' has not been used throughout the chapter.
2. 'Social class' as used here is based on the classification of the Office for Population Census Studies (OPCS), first used in the census of 2001, which updated that of the Registrar General, previously used since 1911. Based on

occupation, lifestyle and status, it is useful here in that it accords with popular understandings of social class differentiation, in particular, the distinctions between white-collar workers on the one hand and blue-collar and those classified as long-term unemployed, on the other. However, it is not without its difficulties. Hill and Cole (2001), for example, have pointed out that it i) masks the existence of the super-rich and the super-powerful (the capitalist class); ii) glosses over and hides the antagonistic and exploitative relationship between the two main classes in society (the capitalist class and the working class); iii) segments the working class and thereby disguises the ultimate common interests of white-collar, blue-collar and long-term unemployed workers (pp. 151–3). Thus, while for the purposes of this chapter, and for sociological analyses in general, it has its uses, its problematic nature should not be forgotten.

3. All names have been changed to protect identity.

References

Baker, D., Street, B. (2001) 'Understandings of Relationships Between Home and School Numeracy Practices: a Report from the Field'. Paper presented at the International Literacy Conference 'Literacy and Language in Global and Local Settings: New Directions for Research and Teaching'. Cape Town.

Bastiani, J. (1989) *Working with Parents. A Whole-school Approach*. Windsor: NFER-Nelson.

Bernstein, B. (1990*) Class, Codes and Control, Vol. 4*. London: Routledge.

Bourdieu, P. (1990) *In Other Words. Essays towards a Reflexive Sociology*. Oxford: Polity Press.

Bourdieu, P. (1991) *Language & Symbolic Power*. Oxford: Polity Press.

Brown, A. (1993) 'Participation, Dialogue and the Reproduction of Social Inequalities', in R. Merttens and J. Vass (eds) *Partnerships in Maths: Parents and Schools. The Impact Project*. London: Falmer Press.

Brown, P. (1997) 'Cultural Capital & Social Exclusion: Some Observations on Recent Trends in Education, Employment, & the Labour Market', in A. Halsey, H. Lauder, P. Brown and A. Wells (eds) *Education, Culture, Economy and Society*. Oxford: Oxford University Press.

Centre for Studies on Inclusive Education (2000) *Index for Inclusion*. CSIE in collaboration with Centre of Educational Needs, University of Manchester; Centre for Educational Research, Canterbury Christ Church College.

Chrispeels, J. (1996) 'Effective Schools and Home School Partnership Roles: a Framework for Parental Involvement', *School Effectiveness and School Improvement*, 7, 297–323.

Department of Education (DES) (1967) *Children & their Primary Schools. A Report of the Central Advisory Council for Education*. London: HMSO.

Department for Education & Science (DfES) (1991) *The Parent's Charter. You and Your Child's Education*. London: HMSO.

Epstein, J. (1995) School/Family/Community Partnerships, *Phi Delta Kappan*, **76** (9) May, 701–711.

Finlay, A. (1999) 'Exploring an Alternative Literacy Curriculum for Socially and Economically Disadvantaged Parents', *UK Journal of Adolescent & Adult Literacy*, September.

Habermas, J. (1973) *Legitimation Crisis*. Oxford: Polity Press.

Hill, D. and Cole, M. (2001) 'Social Class', in D. Hill and M. Cole (eds) *Schooling and Equality: Fact, Concept and Policy*. London: Kogan Page.

Hughes, P. and Macnaughton, G. (2000) 'Consensus, Dissensus or Community: The Politics of Parental Involvement in Early Childhood Education', *Contemporary Issues in Early Childhood*, **1**(3).

Hurley, L. (2000a) 'Education & Equality. Where are we now?' Unpublished.

Hurley, L. (2000b) 'School and parents. The school perspective.' Unpublished.

Lareau, A. (1989) *Home Advantage; Social Class and Parental Intervention in Elementary Education*. London: Falmer Press.

McNamara, O., Hustler, D., Stronach, I. and Rodrigo, M. (2000) 'Room to Manoevre: Mobilising the 'Active Partner' in Home–School Relations', *British Educational Research Journal*, **26**(4), 473–89.

Merttens, R., Newland, A., Webb, S. (1996) *Learning in Tandem. Involving Parents in Their Children's Education*. Warwickshire: Scholastic.

OFSTED (1999) *Primary Education. A Review of Primary Schools in England 1994–98*. London: OFSTED.

Pollard, A. and Filer, A. (1996) *The Social world of Children's Learning*. London: Cassell.

Pugh, G. (1989). 'Parents and Professionals in Pre-school Services: Is Partnership Possible?' in S. Wolfendale (ed.) *Parental Involvement. Developing Networks between School, Home & Community*. London: Cassell.

Reay, D. (1995) 'They Employ Cleaners To Do That. Habitus in the Primary School', *British Journal of the Sociology of Education*, **16**(3), 353.

Reay, D. (1999) *Class Work: Mothers' Involvement in Their Children's Primary Schooling*. London: University College Press.

Sammons, P., Hillman, J. and Mortimore, P. (1995) *Key Characteristics of Effective Schools*. London: OFSTED.

Street, B. (1995) *Social Literacies: Critical Approaches to Literacy in Development, Ethnography and Education*. London: Longman.

Teacher Training Agency (TTA) (2002) *Qualifying to Teach: Professional Standards for Qualified Teacher Status and Requirements for Initial Teacher Training*. London: DfES.

Tizard, B., Mortimore, J. and Burchell, B. (1981) *Involving Parents in Nursery & Infant Schools*. London: High Scope Press.

Vincent, C. (1996) *Parents and Teachers. Power and Participation*. London: Falmer Press.

Walkerdine, V. and Lucey, H. (1989) *Democracy in the Kitchen*. London: Virago.

CHAPTER 5

Community education

Krishan Sood

Introduction

Under the Professional Standards for the award of Qualified Teacher Status document (Teacher Training Agency (TTA) 2002), those awarded Qualified Teacher Status (QTS) (section 1.5) must understand and uphold the professional code of the General Teaching Council for England by demonstrating that they can contribute to, and share responsibility in, the corporate life of schools (p. 6). The use of the term, 'corporate' reflects the present Government's preoccupation with the 'businessification' of education, both with respect to the business agenda *for* schools (meeting the needs of industry) and the business agenda *in* schools (controlling aspects of education and using schooling to make profits) (e.g. Cole 1998a; Hatcher and Hirrt 1999; Rikowski 2002; Hill forthcoming).

This chapter takes the position that schools should properly be thought of as communities rather than corporations. It aims, therefore, to fulfil the TTA requirements, but in a critical way, and specifically it will review some of the issues involved around community education. The chapter is directed at Newly Qualified Teachers (NQTs) and student teachers, but it is also relevant to teachers generally. The term 'community' as opposed to the 'corporate life of the school' encompasses a much wider notion of schools, viewing them as acting as catalysts in bringing the community together. This chapter attempts to explain 'community education' and its potential benefits: it presents a policy framework, and covers some of the organisational and resources issues. It goes on to consider some practical approaches by which NQTs can make a useful contribution to wider school practices and concludes with an overview of the roles and responsibilities of Governors.

Developing community knowledge

While government educational initiatives come and go, the underlying problems of most (inner) cities – mass unemployment, poverty, a mismatch between local skills and new jobs, a declining infrastructure and a low quality of life for many citizens

– have remained, and indeed have intensified over the last two decades. There has been a changing educational landscape over this time period and many of the recent changes in educational policy have been swift and far-reaching. The 1988 Education Act revolutionized the education system and led to far-reaching structural changes in all sectors of education through early years settings, Primary and Secondary schools, sixth-form colleges and further education. It added a new vocabulary of targets, SATs, performance management, advanced skills teachers and so on to the old vocabulary of aims and objectives and educational achievement. It could be argued that the community at large felt inadequate somehow in supporting their children and schools, and had no forum to be engaged in this new debate and, therefore, were not in a position to fight for their rights and entitlements.

Education lays the foundation of a rewarding and successful life, and pupils should be encouraged to take full advantage of the available educational facilities. In one county in which the author worked, making this a reality for the community involved the schools, the community, the LEA and others in jointly addressing such issues as: access to education and progression; a representative higher education system; underachievement; the exclusion rate; motivation; and parent/carer responsibilities and involvement.

Making the educational service more accessible and more relevant are laudable aims for most LEAs, but in the short term, they are unlikely to be entirely acceptable or entirely relevant to everyone. Examples of good practice by LEAs include having systems in place to monitor service provision, access, appropriateness and delivery to people's needs. A supposition here is that individual community members understand how to access such a resource and have the necessary skills and power to negotiate access to key decision-makers. Vincent (1993) considers that a 'statist reform' (p. 367) model of community education, that is to say the emphasis is in attempting to improve and reform state provision, has at its heart the notion of engendering a community spirit, to make available the school's resources and facilities for local residents and to create a sense of shared values and beliefs. Vincent (1993) fails to say what constitutes this 'community', and that community education is a much more complex concept than access to resources. In addition, one needs to ask whose values and beliefs are being considered? If common glue binding schools and communities is not strong enough, then this could mean that schools and their communities have enormous potential either to exacerbate divisions or help build a consensus of support among members who, on other issues, may hold widely divergent views. Rizvi (1993) asserts that in a free market, the consensus between clients and producers will remain little more than a rhetoric of 'romantic localism' (p. 380), where there is a resolute effort to make more palatable a system that is increasingly controlled by the centre.

It is crucial then for a Newly Qualified Teacher (NQT) to take these issues on board and develop an understanding and involvement in a comprehensive and cohesive programme of collaboration and liaison. As past chair of the Race Equality Council's Youth and Education committee, the author participated in a conference involving the voluntary sector, the Local Authority representatives from the education and social services, police and health sector and representatives from the community across Warwickshire. A report was published highlighting some of the major issues (see the Warwickshire Ethnic Minority Community Forum Report 1994) which stemmed mainly from the real needs of the community, the questions that they wanted to raise: it was *their* agenda. As NQTs, can you envisage a role in developing knowledge of the community served by your school through some of the following opportunities?

- Aligning the LEA Curriculum that takes fully into account the profile and the needs of the local population.
- Preparing strong guidelines, setting goals and developing systems that are commensurate with combating racism, poverty and other manifestations of the oppression that their communities face.
- Adopting an enabling role where consultation with young people (young women and young men) is improved to share experiences.
- Ensuring that the major decision-making organisations are adequately represented to avoid powerless talking-shops.
- Working with Asian, black and other minority ethnic youth workers to liaise effectively with minority youth.
- Developing an understanding of Governors' roles and responsibilities, especially in encouraging greater participation from the Asian, black and other minority communities.
- Ensuring a closer liaison with local race equality councils.
- Planning and delivering a curriculum which ensures that languages and cultures remain alive.
- Taking into account parent/carer views when providing extra-curricular activities, particularly in multicultural schools.
- Considering cultural and social factors with respect to the education of multi-lingual pupils.
- Lobbying to ensure there is a permanent meeting place with decent facilities and adequate funding for all community users.

(Adapted from the Warwickshire Ethnic Minority Community Forum Report 1994)

What do we mean by community education?

Community education is much wider than the range of statutory provision which education services generally provide. Community education is certainly about access to educational opportunities for individuals or groups. It is about the concept of building the confidence of communities so they may thrive. The central notion of *confidence* is crucial to the successful development of the individual and to the social cohesiveness of communities. All manner of good things flow from communities that are secure and confident. It is preferable to think of community education as building confidence rather than as meeting the needs of communities. The aims of meeting community needs are laudable but it is doubtful whether we will ever be able, or indeed wish, to obtain an objective measure of an individual's potential or of a community's needs.

Within the education service the youth worker, the adult educator, and the college and university lecturer surely have as much to contribute to community education as the teacher in early years settings does. The important contributions made by the many bodies in the voluntary sector must also not be overlooked. Some community needs are very special and remind us forcibly of the dangers of appearing as 'one bearing gifts'; the author is thinking particularly of the West Indian Community Centre in Derby where their understanding of building confidence was such that the author invariably listened to black friends there rather than advise them.

There have been many attempts to define what is meant by community education. Warwickshire County Council's consultation paper on community education (March 1989) offers this definition: 'Community Education is a method of delivering an education system that creates access to opportunities for personal and community development, and participation by all members of the community in a process of life long education' (p. 2). Community education could not be described by listing activities, as it is more an attitude or approach to the delivery of education and where the capacity to build confidence between different agencies can be catalysed.

Benefits of community education

Some of the community education activities might include the following:

- Shared use of school facilities e.g. swimming pools
- Adult education classes
- Youth clubs and activities
- Provision of meals for the poor and elderly on school or college sites
- Summer play schemes

Those local authorities with substantial experience in the development of community education have noted these benefits:

- It helps people to improve their educational skills, knowledge and qualifications.
- It acts as a generating force in community life.
- It improves the relationships between schools/colleges and their communities.
- It represents the public, providing a wider range of specialist educational services.
- It increases pride in community resources and reduces vandalism.

(Adapted from 'Education for the Whole Community', consultation paper by Warwickshire County Council 1989)

A policy framework

Every community has a wealth of resources, both physical and human. This includes clubs, libraries, teachers, teaching assistants, school classrooms, sports facilities, youth workers, public houses, retired people, experts and so on. They all have a role to play in a 'collaborative' approach. The community school is ideally placed to act as a centrepiece offering advice, information, resources and expertise. The school should not see the community as a resource to fill empty rooms, but rather the school is a resource to support the community. In a community school situated in a multicultural community in which the author taught, every effort was taken to ensure that the community perspective was reflected in the school's approach. With involvement and planning with the community representatives in the curriculum and pastoral areas for example, the school soon offered a range of opportunities with the aim to develop community skills, knowledge and capacities regardless of age, gender, disability, social status or ethnic origin. As NQTS, you can seek to take advantage of such opportunities as:

- Getting directly involved in the development of provision in the locality through establishing 'friendly' groups that meet regularly, somewhere in the community.
- Influencing decision-making through active representation and lobbying in the LEA's strategic plan.
- Having a regular, well-distributed and attractive community newspaper as a forum and lynchpin to coordinate activities and meetings.
- Having regular and well-reported meetings of local committees, councils and so on.
- Having regular social events; often it is easier to raise problems and discuss needs in a social situation.
- Breaking down traditional barriers and 'opening up' the school to the community.
- Establishing close cooperation of all providers and community agencies, whether voluntary or statutory.
- Monitoring, market research and establishing local networks through which unmet needs may be identified.
- Seeking support, guidance and information from an informed and trained staff.

(From author's personal experiences).

Organisational and resources issues

There are a number of possible organisational structures for the provision of community education under the Education Reform Act (1988) and different LEAs have tried different models. These include an authority-led model where certain functions are under a central management structure and an institution-led model. In the latter, all community education might be institutionally mounted, managed and resourced. Another possibility is a local community council where the local community decides priorities. Whichever model is chosen or if there is a mixture, there will still be a legitimate role for an LEA at least in terms of strategic planning, the allocation of resources, and the monitoring and evaluation of delivery.

NQTs – making useful contributions to wider school policies

Effective communication is an important feature of effective schools and colleges. Equally significant is the art of negotiation in communication where the message has to be fully received, accepted by the recipients concerned and acted upon. Tensions arise when the communication is not seen as a two-way exchange, but as a directive from above, without seeking an individual person's views. Staff meetings can be vital arenas for a two-way exchange of ideas and information but much is dependent on whether a bureaucratic or collegial mode (Bush 1994) of management characterises the organisation.

Weber (1947) argued that bureaucracy is the most efficient form of management, which Livingstone (1974) considers is an almost inevitable consequence of increasing size and complexity: 'as organizations grow and become more complex, more formal systems of regulation replace informal understanding that is often sufficient for effective co-ordination in the smaller, simpler units' (p. 9). What this means is that as a NQT you may find a hierarchical authority structure with formal chains of command between the different positions in the hierarchy. This suggests that power resides at the apex of the pyramid with heads having the authority by virtue of their position. This top-down view of educational management may be appropriate at certain times, and for certain reasons, but it remains an ambiguous notion where a collegial approach is the dominant management style. As a NQT you will have to be aware of the need to assess the tension between professionalism and hierarchy. Bush (1994) contests that teachers have the subject expertise which may come into conflict with the positional authority of the head. This seems to go against the Weberian thinking where democratic control may lie with the subject specialists and democratic decisions could well be made by ALL staff in the school, as was the practice in some Inner London Education Authority (ILEA) schools in the 1970s.

Staff meetings in Primary and Secondary schools then remain an open arena where teachers and NQTs can undertake such activities as to:

- Briefly discuss behavioural issues in each class (where pupils with behaviour difficulties are discussed).
- Allow each subject coordinator/head of department to offer feedback on any progress or initiatives which are forthcoming so that all staff are aware.
- Allocate or delegate responsibilities for forthcoming events to staff, thus requiring an input from and the support of all staff.

As NQTs you will have to engage with others in curriculum planning and development meetings in such ways as:

- Being given responsibility for planning a particular area of the curriculum for the following week, or to sharing ideas for festivities such as harvest time or Divali.
- Clarifying the activities that support staff/parent/carer helpers will be doing the following week, and communicating appropriately to them.
- Liaising with outside agencies, e.g. local community leaders, trade union officials, local business people, the vicar, Imam or other people that the children are learning about at the time.
- Visiting teachers in other schools to share ideas of good practice.

Effective teamwork is an ideal to aim for but it may not be a readily attainable norm in many schools. Coleman and Bush (1994) explore how teamwork might be developed and highlight the notion of interdependence between managing with teams and development for those teams. Some of the ways of encouraging collaborative work and learning associated with effective teamwork could be through the use of quality circles (FEU 1989) for staff development. The FEU (1989) suggest the purpose of quality circles is:

> that small volunteer groups of workers meet for an hour a week with a trained leader, operating to a strict code of conduct, to consider work related problems and recommend solutions which are then implemented, unless there are good reasons for not doing so. (FEU 1989: 1)

Based on their experience of learning networks in Enfield LEA, Goddard and Clinton (1994) argue that developments can be better fostered where there is interaction and collaboration between organisations. As NQTs you will have to sharpen your interpersonal skills, leadership and communication ability to make the teamwork process successful through knowledge of the 'curriculum players and pressure groups', those who are usually curriculum managers, heads of departments in secondary schools or colleges, and in primary schools, usually the Senior Management Team (SMT) (Lofthouse 1994: 143). Indeed, teaching staff are not the only stakeholders in a school; there are other individuals like the support staff and Governors who carry the reputation of the school through the local community and are good allies as team members. Curriculum planning is based on the premise of a culture of collaboration (Nias *et al.* 1989) and a culture of support where openness and valuing of group work can be seen to lead to self-confidence within the school. Within such an environment, a NQT can flourish, but in the context of being mindful of the constraints and opportunities of being in a team.

Involvement in school activities

As NQTs within the early years settings, Primary, Secondary, or further education and sixth-form colleges, you will be expected to contribute to a whole range of internal and external activities connected with the institution. To enhance the teaching and learning process, schools must find new allies and build new connections to the community of which they are a part. The development of an effective home and community curriculum based on learning partnerships with parents and carers, as co-educators of children in parallel with teachers/lecturers, is advocated by Brighouse and Woods (1999). NQTs can be catalysts in such partnerships and thereby strengthen the capacity of a school to provide effective learning. This could be through holding open weeks around such topics as the teaching of reading and numeracy at which parents can understand and participate in the learning process involved, and support their children appropriately. You may be able to foster links with other important agencies of community involvement which support teaching and learning, such as service and business providers, to develop a greater economic understanding, an awareness of the world of work and of the nature of citizenship. Some business volunteers help Secondary schools/colleges with their Young Enterprise programmes and work through Education Business Partnerships. However, liaisons with business should be conducted in the spirit of critical enquiry, and the views of workers and trade union representatives should be sought as well as those of official business spokespersons. Links with local public libraries are a further boost to teaching and learning through homework and independent study. The provision of curriculum enrichment and extension opportunities provide a real opportunity to prepare for lifelong learning. Extra-curricular provision is defined in a DfEE (1997) report entitled *School Performance and Extra Curricular Provision*:

1. *Curriculum enrichment:* traditional extra-curricular activities such as sport, drama, chess, photography and other clubs and societies.
2. *Curriculum extension:* study opportunities provided before or after school or during the breaks in the school day, such as homework clubs, extra revision classes and extra after-school tuition, whether undertaken voluntarily or as the result of teacher direction.
3. *Homework:* work set in lessons, integral to the curriculum, to be done either at home or in curriculum extension time at school.

(DfEE 1997)

A further DfEE publication in 1998, entitled *Extending Opportunity: A National Framework for Study Support*, defines study support *as* 'learning activity outside normal lessons which young people take part in voluntarily' (p. 3). What is very important for schools and colleges is that good practice in curriculum enrichment and extension are carefully monitored by age, gender and ethnicity and to ensure that there is a large proportion of staff involvement and as NQTs you will encourage participation by as many pupils as possible.

A number of Secondary schools have homework clubs, breakfast clubs, subject surgeries, study weeks, Easter revision programmes for Year 11 pupils, summer literacy schools and help with key skills (Brighouse and Woods 1999). Similarly, Primary schools have developed 'Early Bird' (Brighouse and Woods 1999: 101) schemes for children who want to be in school early.

Looking through the annual calendar of events, one can see a whole host of school functions which may make demands on your time. The main theme of community education is that education is a partnership between home and school. Home visiting is one way to establish a strong bond between pupils, parents and the school community. Home visiting recognises, values and builds on the principle that parents/carers are the first educators of their child. For example, in the early years setting, you may be asked to make home visits prior to admissions to explain procedures and allay any parental/carers' fears. It is important that a programme of home visits starts with discussions with all staff to agree principles and procedures and that everyone is aware of the various needs, attitudes and values of a pluralist community. As NQTs, you will need to consult and involve other colleagues like multilingual assistants in your preparation, and ensure that you are giving sensitive and jargon-free messages. One good example on how to do a home visit is through a paired visit where one person talks with parents/carers while the colleague plays and talks with the children, all the time, being sensitive to parents'/carers' feelings so the presence of two 'professionals' is not threatening.

Your expertise and experience, in addition to enthusiasm and energy might have to be channelled through involvement in areas like: parents'/carers' evenings, school councils, sporting events, Parent-Teacher Association, school trips, prize-giving events and school plays and rehearsals. In a Primary school, each class usually has to contribute towards the school assembly, to share the ongoing work of the classes and to celebrate the learning across the school. Parents/carers are invited to class assemblies or end-of-term concerts, so NQTs may have an opportunity to join in. You may find yourself involving parents/carers, Governors and community leaders to help in fund-raising or the school sports day. In the myriad of extra-curricular activities, a NQT can be called on to assist in running a club like arts, chess, craft, gardening and to liaise with outside agencies in the production of whole school exhibitions or concerts. For example, if you run a football club, you might wish to involve the local football team or to arrange inter-school football matches or inter-house or inter-form hockey matches. If there is an active involvement in arranging fieldtrips, school visits or residential experience, then your expertise or just your presence as an extra adult may prove to be very welcome. Parents/carers' evenings are a very important element of the home–school partnership. Having displays that show work for all areas of the curriculum, including photographs and diaries of visits, adds to the variety and best shows off the institution to the community. In one Infant school, each Governor was assigned to a teacher as a partner, e.g. a Governor keen on IT was assigned to the IT coordinator, thus building partnerships in different ways.

Some of the negative aspects of getting involved with so many activities can be attributed to some of the following factors:

- Lack of time to liaise with outside agencies and arrange events owing to full teaching timetables, and lack of non-contact time (in the early years and Primary school setting specifically).

- Lack of money for supply cover for when you want to go and see teachers in other schools.
- Constraints of the curriculum and timetable which limit flexibility.
- Perceived lack of support and advice from the SMT regarding liaising with particular outside agencies.

Whatever the expertise of a NQT, it is important to demonstrate that some kind of contribution is being made to the welfare of the school and its community.

Roles and responsibilities of Governors

The role and responsibilities of Governors in maintained schools in England are wide and varied (see Drayton 1999 and the DfES 2002 Governors' website). Recent inspection evidence has shown that where there is an active involvement by governing bodies in their school's planning, Governors are better informed and more effective in assisting the school to progress (OFSTED 1994). The Education Reform Act of 1988 gave Governors responsibility for the school's budget, once financial delegation had occurred. It also gave Governors power and duties with regard to the appointment and dismissal of staff. *School Governors: a Guide to the Law* (DfE 1994) defines the responsibilities of school governing bodies as: 'helping to establish (with the head) the aims and policies of the school, and how the standards of education can be improved' (DfE 1994: 15). In the paper on *Governing Bodies and Effective Schools* (BIS/DfE/OFSTED 1995: 2), the emphasis is on a strategic view, with monitoring and evaluation of a school's effectiveness being promoted.

The duties of governing bodies also encapsulate accountability. The governing body is accountable to parents through its annual report and annual parents'/carers' meeting. It is also is accountable to the local authority, to OFSTED and to the local community. In turn, staff are accountable to the governing body. (See DfES 2002 Governors' website for further details on accountability of Governors.)

Giving time to the school and sharing tasks among the Governors are often some of the important features of an effective governing body. However, as Corrick (1996) notes, Governors often shy away from entering into a debate on school improvement or strategy to improve standards of education because some feel intimidated or underskilled in tackling such issues. Instead, there is a tendency for Governors to become involved in matters with which they feel familiar and comfortable. It could be that some head teachers are reluctant to allow Governors to get involved in the day-to-day running of the school. Governors need support and guidance to work collaboratively with all those who make contact with a school. They need to feel self-assured that they are *asking the right questions* and *the way in which such questions are asked* is an important indicator of good school–Governor relationships. Sometimes tensions arise with teachers and Governors when each other's roles are unclear or there is an assumption that one party has more 'power' than the other. This is an opportunity for Governors not to feel inhibited about questioning the judgements of teachers or becoming blinded by educational jargon. Both Governors and teachers (including NQTs) have a crucial role to play in shaping the future direction of a school. Corrick (1996) argues that taking ownership of the vision of the future of a school demands a high level of skills, knowledge and confidence on the part of Governors. A kind of detachment is required at times from immediate concerns, in order to look at all the options from different viewpoints. This is a piece of advice NQTs would do well to bear in mind. As an NQT, you can contribute to the development of improvement within a school by working alongside Governors, sharing your vision with them, sharing and reflecting on good practice to raise awareness and collaborating on planning activities. Creese (1998) adds caution that where there are weaknesses to be addressed within a school, then there has to be 'a high level of mutual trust between governors and staff' (p. 123), so that those weaknesses can be dealt with frankness and openness.

As a past advisory teacher, the author was privileged to be involved in supporting clusters of Primary schools in curriculum development, INSET and policy development. In one cluster made up of three Infant and Junior schools' governing bodies, a presentation on the development of a multicultural policy was given. After the governors had accepted the much broader definition of multicultural education, it was easier to explain that multicultural education should be seen as a process which permeates the curriculum, rather than something added on as an afterthought or as something which looks only at the strange and exotic. Stress was laid on developing attitudes of justice, tolerance and respect rather than on contrived references to the minority ethnic communities.[1] Good practice within the classroom was one of the starting points for discussion and there was debate on the need for a multicultural policy, how to develop it further, how to support staff in resourcing, what to monitor, how to reach out to the parents and how to measure the success of the policy's impact on learning and attainment. Success of this training lay in knowing the schools well, enjoying a good relationship with the staff and pupils, collaboration and teamwork and helping to target a specific need and training requirements of the staff. The important message for a NQT here is that you should continue to form close and frequent contacts with all those who are in contact with the school – parents, Governors, advisers, learning support staff, health visitors and others. This requires development of good channels of communication, openness, trust and mutual respect for institutional improvement. Creese (1998), in his research, notes that in one Secondary school a retired head was brought in to lead team-building sessions for the governing body. This then turned into a viable and regular induction programme for new Governors.

Conclusion

I have argued that schools/colleges and other educational settings should be considered as communities rather than as corporations. Community education is treated above as a complex concept and the notion of building community confidence is put forward as the central focus of what community education means. Emphasis is put on building relationships, partnerships and liaisons with different stakeholders, and within this, confidence in each other is called for. The chapter has considered some practical strategies for NQTs with respect to their getting involved in the daily and extra-curricular activities in the variety of educational sectors and has concluded with raising awareness about the complexity of the roles and responsibilities of governing bodies.

Note

1. Various critiques of multicultural education abound in the following authors' work: Troyna (ed.) (1987), Brown (1988), Tomlinson, (1990), Cole (1998b) and May (ed.) (1999). These authors have critiqued a concept of multicultural education based solely on cultural artefacts and some (e.g. Brown (1988), Cole (1998b) and Troyna (1987)) have argued that it should be replaced by antiracist education (which takes the undermining of racism as the primary aim). Multicultural education has also been critiqued by those who favour monocultural education (education promoting so-called 'British values') against the cultural diversity stressed in multicultural education. My own view is that multicultural education should be retained but critically reviewed through the discourse of power and inequality and that it should complement antiracist education.

References

BIS/DfE/OFSTED (1995) *Governing Bodies and Effective Schools.* London: Standards in Education, DfE.

Brighouse, T. and Woods, D. (1999) *How to Improve Your School.* London: Routledge.

Brown, C. (1988) 'The White Highlands: Multiculturalism and Antiracism', *Multiculturalism Teaching,* 6(2), 38–9.

Bush, T. (1994) 'Theory and Practice in Educational Management', in T. Bush and J. West-Burnham (eds) *The Principles of Educational Management.* Harlow: Longman.

Cole, M. (1998a) 'Globalisation, Modernisation and Competitiveness: a critique of the New Labour project in education', *International Studies in Sociology of Education,* 8(3), 315–32.

Cole, M. (1998b) 'Racism, Reconstructed Multiculturalism and Antiracist Education', *Cambridge Journal of Education,* 28(1), March 1998, 37–48.

Coleman, M. and Bush, T. (1994) 'Managing with Teams', in T. Bush and J. West-Burnham (eds) *The Principles of Educational Management.* Harlow: Longman.

Corrick, M. (1996) 'Effective Governing Bodies, Effective Schools?,' in P. Earley, B. Fidler and J. Ouston *Improving through Inspection?* London: David Fulton Publishers.

Creese, M. (1998) 'The Strategic Role of Governors in School Improvement', in D. Middlewood and J. Lumby (eds) *Strategic Management in Schools and Colleges*. London: Paul Chapman Publishing.

DfE (1994) *School Governors: A Guide to the Law*. London: HMSO.

DfEE (1997) *School Performance and Extra Curricular Provision*. London: DfEE.

DfEE (1998) *Extending Opportunity: a National Framework for Study Support*. London: DfEE.

Department for Education and Skills (DfES) (2002) School Governors' Gateway, http://www.dfes.gov.uk/schoolgovernors/index.shtml (accessed 8 May 2002).

Drayton, M. (1999) 'The Role and Purpose of School Governing Bodies', in M. Cole (ed.) *Professional Issues for Teachers and Student Teachers*. London: David Fulton Publishers.

FEU (Further Education Unit) (1989) *An Evaluation of Quality Circles in Colleges of FE*, Planning Staff Development, number 7. London: FEU.

Goddard, D. and Clinton, B. (1994) 'Learning Networks', in S. Ransom and J. Tomlinson (eds) *School Co-Operation: New Forms of Local Governance*. Harlow: Longman.

Hatcher, R. and Hirrt, N. (1999) 'The Business Agenda behind Labour's Education Policy', in M. Allen, C. Benn, C. Chitty, M. Cole, R. Hatcher, N. Hirrt and G. Rikowski (eds) *Business, Business, Business: New Labour's Education Policy*. London: Tufnell Press

Hill, D. 'Global Capital, Neo-liberalism, and Education Policy: the Growth of Educational Inequality' (forthcoming).

Livingstone, H. (1974) *The University: An Organizational Analysis*. Glasgow: Blackie.

Lofthouse, M. (1994) 'Managing the Curriculum', in T. Bush. and J. West-Burnham (eds) *The Principles of Educational Management*. Harlow: Longman.

May, S. (ed.) (1999) *Critical Multiculturalism: Rethinking Multicultural and Anti-racist Education*. London: Falmer Press.

Nias, J., Southworth, G. and Yeomans, R. (1989) *Staff Relationships in the Primary School*. London: Cassell.

OFSTED (1994) *Improving Schools*. London: HMSO.

Rikowski, G. (2002) *Schools: Building for Business*. London: Tufnell Press.

Rizvi, F. (1993) 'Williams on Democracy and the Governance of Education', in D. Dworkin and L. Roman (eds) *Views Beyond the Border Country: Raymond Williams and Cultural Politics*. London: Routledge.

Tomlinson, S. (1990) *Multicultural Education in the White School*. London: Batsford.

Troyna, B. (ed.) (1987) *Racial inequality in Education*. London: Tavistock Publication.

Teacher Training Agency (TTA) (2002) *Qualifying to Teach: Professional Standards for Qualified Teacher Status and Requirements for Initial Teacher Training*. London: DfES.

Vincent, C. (1993) 'Education for the Community', *British Journal of Educational Studies*, 41(4), 366–80.

Warwickshire County Council (1989) *Education for the Whole Community – Consultation Paper on Warwickshire's Proposals for the Development of Community Education.* Warwickshire County Council. (March).

Warwickshire Ethnic Minority Community Forum Report (1994) *A Special Need to Consult, Summary Report of Consultation Seminars.* Warwickshire Ethnic Minority Community Forum.

Weber, M. (1947) in T. Parsons (ed.) *The Theory of Social and Economic Organization.* Glencoe, IL: Free Press and New York: Collier-McMillan.

CHAPTER 6

Teachers and other professionals

Krishan Sood

Introduction

Under the Professional Standards for the Award of Qualified Teacher Status document (Teacher Training Agency (TTA) 2002a), those awarded qualified teacher status (QTS) (section 1.6) must understand and uphold the professional code of the General Teaching Council for England by demonstrating that they understand the contribution that support staff and other professionals make to teaching and learning. This chapter offers insight into some of the issues involved in forming collaborations with different people and organisations and is aimed at the Newly Qualified Teachers (NQTs) specifically, although it is relevant to teachers generally. Schools differ in very many ways, although each can demonstrate a shared sense of collegiality (Bush 1994), as is evident in the way the teachers and other professionals such as teaching assistants and learning mentors relate to their pupils. Schools and education departments in universities are continuing to explore ways of deploying these staff so that more effective use is made of their abilities and their curricular and pastoral strengths. The DfEE publication, *Teachers: Meeting the Challenges of Change* (1998), states that:

> Teaching and learning can be strengthened by using the full potential of teaching assistants and school support staff . . . teaching assistants are playing an increasingly important role in school on tasks such as literacy support and helping pupils/students with special educational needs . . . we want that contribution to be fully acknowledged for the first time . . . (DfEE 1998: 55–6)

Although the DfEE acknowledges the contribution of 'other support staff', it falls short of explaining what their role is, nor is there any analysis of the effectiveness of it.

As NQTs you will have to learn to establish effective collaborative working relationships with experienced teachers, learning support staff and other professionals such as parents/carers, psychologists, librarians, learning mentors, personal advisers and others responsibile for pupils' education or welfare, such as school administrative staff, and adults working with aspects of PSHE, such as sex and relationships and drugs education (TTA 2002b: 7). Effective relationships in schools are fostered where there is a conducive learning environment and where people feel that they are listened to, are valued and regarded as worthwhile individuals by pupils, parents, Governors and staff. Mortimore *et al.* (1994), however, found that the voices of associate staff were seldom heard, an image which tends to distort the balance of relationships that exists in schools. It is therefore important for NQTs to understand how the structures, systems and interpersonal relationships operate in schools, how certain groups might be excluded and how, if this is the case, one should move towards their inclusion.

Over the past few years there has been an increase in the number of learning support assistants that schools employ (Bell 2000). In a study by Noble (2002) of an analysis of the cost-effectiveness of the employment of associate staff in a Primary school, a high value was placed on the work of learning support assistants by staff, children and parents. They were thought to represent excellent value for money.

It is worth remembering as a NQT that the work of the learning support assistants is more likely to be effective if their role is made clear. You could do this by making your expectations of LSAs and of the pupils clear and precise. The learning support assistants can be given copies of weekly planning at the beginning of each week and the teacher and the LSA should find time – say, if released from assembly on Monday – to discuss the planning and where possible, to incorporate lists of resources needed throughout the week so that these can be prepared in advance. Ainscow (2000) throws doubt on the benefits of the use of learning support assistants in classrooms, suggesting that there can be tensions and barriers built between children who are and are not supported, thus preventing development of good relations. But further research is needed to establish if learning support assistants do make a difference in classrooms (see McPherson 1997; Crowther *et al.* 1998). The Green Paper, *14–19 Extending Opportunities, Raising Standards* (DfES 2002a) emphasises the need to increase the number of learning support assistants in schools and colleges.

How adults/professionals work in school

There are many professionals and volunteers who help and support in schools. In one Secondary school, effective collaboration between a NQT and a mentor was established where both have ensured that their working relationship operates smoothly. In a Primary school, a school policy for work with social workers, educational psychologists, education welfare officers, youth justice and health professionals and others, has been written and accessed by all, rather than each member of staff having to devise their own ways to manage their working relationship.

Schools operate as 'open' organisations, subject to pressures and influences from the wider environment (Coleman *et al.* 1994). They are becoming more pro-active in making links with other agencies, like education welfare officers and health professionals. The links between schools and external advisers and support personnel need careful management. In turbulent times, for example, a school needs to be 'flexible and adaptive' (Hoyle 1986: 98), whereas in a stable environment, a more formal 'mechanistic' model may be most effective. Additionally, with schools forming a range of relationships with people, they are increasingly called to be accountable.

Accountability, as discussed by Scott (1989), may be multifaceted and could involve public accountability, professional accountability or consumerist accountability. NQTs should be able to identify examples of all three types of accountability in their establishments. Within the normative concept of professional accountability, for example, stress is upon the accountability of teachers to their profession. It is linked with self-reporting or self-evaluation, but may involve some level of dialogue with interested parties. This type of accountability would not appear to be totally compatible with responsiveness to the customer in a market environment. In planning a collaborative partnership with other professionals, the notion of accountability to parents, pupils and other stakeholders is crucial. So the need to understand each other's role and differing responsibilities is vital for a NQT. In analysing the needs of a Special Educational Needs (SEN) child through observations and notes made, you could refer to an experienced staff member first and then, with their help and guidance, become involved with the SEN coordinator. For anything more serious, for example in cases of suspected abuse, you need to consult an identified person, usually the head teacher (see Chapter 9).

An understanding of the roles and responsibilities of different professionals in meeting the needs of pupils is an important element of teaching. Not only do you have to know who to call on, like social workers, educational psychologists, education welfare officers, youth justice and health professionals, but you also need to be aware of the systems which exist to support you. You may also find that the school has a range of communication networks with voluntary agencies. It is therefore essential to be pro-active and strategic in collaborating with a range of professionals in order to reduce the likelihood of duplication (Sweeney 1999).

Establishing relationships

The key to collaboration with a range of people within different environments lies in forming lasting relationships. Relationship marketing (Payne *et al.* 1995) seems an especially helpful perspective and approach to be considered for schools in this collaboration. This concept recognises that marketing is about a relationship built over time between individual people inside and outside the organisation, and not a distant, impersonal link between the 'customer' and the 'corporation' (Stokes 1996). It seems that such an approach to external links characterises much of what primary and secondary schools have attempted to do for many years for sound 'educational' purposes, without the word 'marketing' being mentioned. Whether such a view of marketing is accepted or rejected, it seems that most schools are actually rather good at it.

Effective working relationships with others, then, requires teachers having an overview about the roles and responsibilities of all the partners. In one school, all staff had a list of professionals associated with the school and knew their reasons for being involved.

It is necessary therefore for NQTs to get involved in the development phase, be it planning, team teaching, evaluating a project or disseminating information, but always ensuring it is done in a collegial fashion. You can take an opportunity to involve other adults in this process across all stages of the education phase. For example, being actively involved in the foundation stage may involve some of these approaches:

- Liaising with teachers to gain informal reports on the pupils.
- Discussing with members of staff the simplest way of completing standard assessment sheets, which can be passed throughout the school to maintain continuity and progression.
- Taking responsibility for a curriculum area, involving liaison with other teachers to ensure the correct delivery of the subject in question.
- Having team planning or briefing meetings on a regular basis, giving everyone the opportunity to discuss any new issues or air any concerns. Furthermore, this also indicates that everyone is following the same plan and working together as a team.

(Observations by Ms Mistry, a classteacher)

Managing the work of generalist teaching assistants, parents, volunteers and/or mentors in the classroom so they can enhance learning opportunities for pupils requires clear objectives for them to work towards. These adults, especially volunteers and parents, also need to work with pupils where they can see progression in pupils' learning and therefore boosting their own self-confidence. As one experienced teacher noted, 'NQTs need to be aware of the need for cooperative planning and through such meetings develop self-confidence and respect from other members of staff' (Ms Mistry, a classteacher).

Working collaboratively with specialist teachers requires meticulous written plans and targets that can be shared easily and communicated effectively. Joint planning with the appropriate adults clarifies and defines roles and outcomes and reduces tensions which may affect learning. If the learning support staff are not involved in planning, then they do not know the reasons for doing a particular activity.

In a busy classroom, the need to manage time effectively is crucial, especially during pupil assessments and record keeping. Encouraging and involving additional adults can ease the task by requesting an adult to help make observations or keep tick lists. Also, talking to them just for a few minutes after the session helps to monitor progress. Such discussions help to foster better working relationships to advance the pupils' learning. In a study of learning support work by Balshaw (1999), it was found that support staff carried out a huge array of tasks, including cataloguing reading books, recording television programmes, liaison and coordinating tasks and so on. As

NQTs, you should understand and acknowledge the wide range of skills and abilities the support staff have in order to maximise these to the benefit of pupil learning.

As NQTs, you are used to being observed when undertaking your teaching practice. Therefore it should not pose too much of a threat to be observed by different staff and to get feedback. You should be able to handle with professionalism constructive criticism and suggestions for improving classroom practice.

Working collaboratively with colleagues in planning, teaching and assessment, inside and outside the classroom, requires professionalism at all times. All members of staff have a key role to play in the education of pupils in a school as well as acting collaboratively with colleagues in pursuance of school or team objectives. Most teachers participate in various types of meetings and take on extra-curricular activities. As a NQT, you can join with an experienced member of staff to run a club if you do not feel confident at doing this independently.

The role of teaching assistants

The school needs to have a clear job description for each type of teaching assistant as their duties will differ from one area to another, and from one Key Stage to another. For example, teaching assistants in Reception may have a different job description to teaching assistants involved in literacy or numeracy in Key Stage 2. In Secondary schools where learning mentors are employed, a range of roles and tasks are undertaken both within and outside a classroom. For example, a learning mentor may be working outside a classroom to produce resources and materials to support learning, or in another role, s/he may be physically escorting pupils to school. Teaching assistants' job descriptions need to be available to the teachers with whom they work so that teachers can give them appropriate tasks.

As NQTs you need to ensure that all adults in the classroom are clear about their respective roles in the lesson. For example, extra adults in the classroom could have photocopies of your planning with their activity highlighted so that they know exactly what they are doing and why. You can make the learning support staff aware of any difficult pupils before the lesson starts so that they can contribute to the positive management of pupils' behaviour or alternatively the learning support staff can let *you* know of problems. The teaching assistants also need to be familiar with the NQT's procedures regarding discipline. In this case it will be easier if there is a whole-school policy regarding discipline, so that all staff are clear. In one school, a method called assertive discipline is used and in the main this works well for most pupils, with the exception being where extreme forms of negative behaviour are exhibited by pupils. Equally important is to reward good behaviour by encouraging, praising and rewarding with special activities.

Shaw's (2001) work on learning supporters show that this group carry out a range of activities under the management of the teacher. They perform tasks like 'spotting early signs of bullying and disruptive behaviour and implementing behaviour management policies' (p. 5). So it is central for all NQTs to work closely with such colleagues so as to draw on their considerable knowledge, understanding, skills and abilities.

Inclusion

Some of the principles and characteristics of inclusive education are based on viewing inclusion as a human rights issue in which a school has no physical, attitudinal or organisational barriers. Inclusion is seen as a human rights issue because all pupils have the right to learn together, where they are not devalued by exclusion and where pupils do not need to be protected from each other if there is a caring environment. Furthermore, social interaction is likely to reduce fear and build friendship, respect and understanding in preparation for their role as emergent active citizens.

As a NQT, you will have to be aware of the different needs of pupils, based on their individuality. All will belong to a social class, an ethnic group, a religious tradition (or none), a gender and a local neighbourhood. Some will have special educational needs and, from a certain age, all will have a sexual identity. So for an inclusive education, you will have to plan to teach for an inclusive, holistic education where all pupils are made to succeed. What seems an important prerequisite for an inclusive environment is the need for all teachers and learning support staff to foster and nurture this, leading to all pupils playing their part in being educated.

To take the issue of disability as an example, some of the practical steps to achieve inclusion for a pupil with a disability could be:

- to conduct an access audit of the school/other environment;
- to ask and involve the pupil in decision-making;
- to discourage negative language;
- to vary teaching and learning approaches to encourage and celebrate diversity;
- to consult and collaborate with statutory agencies, health, social services, educational psychologists, specialist teachers, teaching assistants and parent(s)/carer(s) to promote an inclusive ethos; and
- to develop empowerment and self-representation for disabled pupils.

Additionally, as NQTs, you will need to be involved in disability equality training for staff and governors and understand how to monitor and evaluate the inclusive process. According to Booth *et al.* (2000), inclusion is about fostering mutually sustaining relationships between schools and communities, suggesting that you should form alliances with various people and go on listening and learning from them. Central to this debate is the need for all schools to be able to explain to all what their values and cultures are in developing inclusive practices.

Teachers try to take a pro-active approach to ensure that all pupils are developing a positive sense of identity and self-esteem. As teachers in a classroom learning environment we often try to generate labels which will enable us to group pupils together to make large-sized classes more manageable, for example, 'ability' groups, 'interest' groups and 'friendship' groups. But this strategy carries with it a number of risks.

The label may be inappropriate and/or it may not reflect the pupils' perspectives; the label may fit only in certain situations; pupils may be given very few opportunities to demonstrate change and/or development and the pupil may learn to 'fit' the label even though it was not initially an appropriate one. Labelling pupils does not only affect the learning opportunities offered to them and the relationships they are able to develop and sustain, but will also reflect upon their sense of self-identity and upon their learning behaviours. It is extremely important, therefore, that teachers and other learning support staff use 'labels' sparingly and that the labels they employ are flexible, responsive and regularly updated and reviewed.

Staff who are allocated to support a pupil with specific educational needs or those learning English as an additional language need to be clear about their role. They need to be very clear too about which children they are working with and why, as misunderstandings arise when this is not communicated effectively amongst the staff. Additional support staff may also need to be gently reminded that they are there to help pupils think for themselves, not to encourage dependence. As noted by a Key Stage 2 classteacher, 'they should not to do the work for them'. There has been recent research and inspection findings that confirm the 'tremendous contribution' made by well-managed and well-trained assistants to the learning process (DfEE 2000).

Some of the strategies used to develop a pupil's identity and self-esteem could be:

- Respecting and valuing pupils as individuals and their parent(s) and families in the setting.
- Not doing everything for pupils, but encouraging them to become independent.
- Providing positive images of a diverse society.
- Giving pupils opportunities to identify their own needs, abilities and learning in all areas of development.
- Enabling pupils to build self-image through the recognition of progress as well as attainment.
- Accommodating change and development and resisting the use of stereotypical 'labels' for which there is little or no personal 'evidence'.

Working with parents

Building effective relationships with parents and the community is an important role of all schools. But what is even more crucial is for managers to recognise the importance of managing accessibility of all people so as to maximise the learning opportunity for all pupils. Forming a good, lasting home–school relationship is not simple as parents sometimes feel uneasy in approaching the school, perhaps because of their own experience of schools and schooling. Perceived barriers for some are quite real, and it is up to everyone to help reduce these (see Whalley 2001).

New ways of working with the community have been identified by the work of Whalley (2001). Examples of good practice identified through her Pen Green Centre project (Whalley 2001: 20) on how to work with parents include:

- 'encouraging parents to observe and understand how and what their children are learning at home';
- 'acknowledging the skills and competencies of parents and building on these to enhance our own pedagogical strategies';
- 'encourage parents to feel equal and active in their involvement, and to develop an information exchange as a two-way process'; and
- 'provide accessible and relevant routes into involvement so that all families . . . feel informed about their children's development – for example, fathers as well as mothers, isolated vulnerable parents, and parents who are traditionally "hard to reach"'.

It is important to recognise that it takes time to establish an 'equal, active and responsible partnership' (Whalley 2001: 35) with parents. As NQTs, you may need to develop and extend your people skills by going on courses associated with dealing with parents. Research by Tett *et al.* (2000) have shown that where bilingual and multilingual workers helped parents to feel comfortable with the staff and the school, this helped to foster better relationships (for an extended discussion of the challenge of parental involvement, see Chapter 4 of this volume).

NQTS or even experienced teachers in the Primary sector rarely have non-contact time to reach out to the local community. So additional adults in the classroom are good allies for schools, as they often have a wealth of local knowledge and experience about the community, that can be shared for the benefit of pupils. The challenge is to develop meaningful and a common understanding about their roles within the classroom. When working in a community Secondary school, the author built community confidence by meeting parents in their own homes, understanding their concerns, and developing a language which fostered a common trust. Much more needs to be done by schools to bring closer together the teachers, the new and the experienced, learning support assistants, other professionals and parents to provide quality education.

Working with visiting professionals

The great untapped energy and abilities of other visiting professionals from the community can enhance a school's curriculum and go some way to revitalise staff enthusiasm. The important message is that these visitors should be made to feel valued by the whole school community. There are many good examples like suspending the school's timetable for a week to permeate intercultural activities across the curriculum. So trips to a gurdwara or a synagogue (Sikh and Jewish places of worship respectively) can be made educationally exciting by inviting people from such faiths to raise initial awareness. In three Primary schools, for example, rituals and celebrations formed a project where multicultural dance focused on Chinese New Year Celebrations. A visiting musician, dancer and cultural artist from China enchanted teachers and pupils alike with the sounds of her Ku-Cheng – Chinese Harp. In one county, several Secondary schools had planned the entire term's curriculum round an arts project. In another two Secondary schools, there was collaboration of Year 8 classes focusing on a language week.

There were cross-curricular, cross-phase, cross-art-forms projects, Technology weeks, a composing project with a symphony orchestra and classical singer, traditional folk songs revealing social history, projects with sculptors and photographers creating knowledge and pride of place as well as new skills for pupils and teachers. In all this, there was a sense of energy, commitment, creativity, collaboration, cooperation and celebration.

Working with the Ethnic Minority and Traveller Achievement Grant (EMTAG) teachers

NQTs need to be aware of the role of such specialists as the Ethnic Minority and Traveller Achievement Grant (EMTAG) teachers. The author has specific experience as a past advisory teacher for intercultural education in developing an intercultural support programme permeating a whole school. This involved leading, guiding, teaching and supporting teachers in the classroom to develop the curriculum which was more inclusive, holistic and diverse in its approach. There were activities to support classroom teachers through workshops to develop an anti-racist approach to Science, days of INSET on Arts across the World to raise cultural awareness, Governor training on issues of ethnicity and gender and through short- and long-term projects and residencies developing Dance and Drama programmes, exhibitions and performances. The success of such initiatives was seen through the creativity of teachers in making learning exciting, fun and relevant to a wide variety of pupils, and, ultimately, owning the project or ideas which enhanced the curriculum.

On a practical basis, in every curriculum subject there are opportunities to engage pupils by showing respect for their cultural and personal identities. Here, issues of inequality and injustice can be explored using role play, developing knowledge and understanding of the history and development of one's own cultural traditions and of the ways in which these both foster and constrain one's own personal identity. There has been much borrowing, mingling and mutual influence over the centuries between different countries and cultural traditions. This gives NQTs an opportunity to develop in their pupils an ability to learn from different cultural experiences, norms and perspectives, and to empathise with people of different traditions. Equally important is the development in pupils of the willingness to challenge instances of prejudice, intolerance and discrimination of any kind.

In art, visiting artists and minority ethnic staff can with teachers develop a range of resources stressing cross-cultural borrowings and influences. In English, fiction, drama and poetry can be drawn from a range of genres, times and places. In geography, pupils can be shown practical ways of making global connections and recognising interdependence. In history, British history can be taught within a world perspective, related to events in other countries. In mathematics, activities could be developed to reflect the multi-ethnic and multicultural nature of modern societies. In personal, social and health education, there are opportunities for reflection on events in the school itself, including bullying and racial name-calling. Here, the teacher can stress techniques and methods of conflict resolution which pupils themselves can use. Many more ideas can be found in The Runnymede Trust (1993) (see also Cole *et al.* (eds) (1997) and Hill and Cole (eds) (1999)).

NQTs, then, need to be aware of the role of these specialist teachers and where their support can best fit in the curriculum. Perhaps the EMTAG teachers could join the school planning meetings or see the half-termly plan to offer suggestions on how targeted support can be offered. Experience of working with such support staff and other agencies suggests that NQTs have to be flexible to mutually arrange dates and times of their meetings as these professionals may also have to visit other schools.

Working with the Traveller Education Service

The work of the Traveller Education Service (TES) according to the OFSTED (1996) report is generally of a high standard. The education for traveller children in one Midland County is provided by the West Midlands Consortium Education Service for Travelling Children. Advisory teachers from this establishment have very successfully run courses for BA Primary (QTS) students for a number of years at the author's ITT institution. In one example, an advisory teacher for the travelling children noted that her/his work with gypsy and traveller families involved an holistic service provision, and s/he was not thinking in isolation about accommodation, health care, education and welfare. A family constantly and erratically moved on and disrupted is not in a good position to prioritise preventative health care or education. The role of the travellers' adviser is then to jointly sit down and plan with the different agencies, teachers and in consultation with the Gypsy and Traveller community the best and most cost-effective solutions. As NQTs, you need to understand and plan strategies with other teachers and support staff for the teaching and learning of all pupils, including the travelling pupils. In the OFSTED (1996) report, the need for schools to openly acknowledge and give positive images of the different nomadic communities is emphasised.

As stated earlier, developing good relationships with parents is an essential role of a school. NQTs can develop good practice when meeting and working with new parents, particularly those from the Gypsy/Traveller community, in these ways. Families will expect you to be reliable, positive and sympathetic to their needs and to respect the confidentiality of any information they may give you. It may be that other people's values, lifestyle and experiences may differ from yours but will be equally valid. Be aware of cultural differences, gender roles, child rearing, expectation for education, family responsibilities and work patterns affecting young people. Parents themselves may have little or no experience of school or pre-school opportunities and may not read or write well, if at all. Pens, pencils, books, paper, toys may not be available in the home. School premises may be daunting and educational terminology not readily understood. Children may be late starters at school – 6, 7, 8 or even older – and parents may be reluctant to part from children, especially the youngest. In addition, the value of early years education may not be recognised. (For further information, contact the West Midland Consortium Education Service for Travelling Children, The Graiseley Centre, Pool Street, Wolverhampton, WV2 4NE.)

Working with Special Education Needs coordinators

Knowing how to plan collaboratively with SEN coordinators (SENCOs) and SEN support teachers requires an understanding of their roles. As NQTs, you need to be familiar with the layout and purpose of an Individual Education Plan (IEP). Sometimes the learning support assistants work more closely with children with special educational needs and may well have important contributions to make to their IEPs. The inclusion of these colleagues in making plans signals recognition of their valuable support.

The need for each learning support colleague to know what they are going to do everyday is an important management function of the NQT. These adults should know, through regular patterns of meetings, where they are going to be, which pupils they will be working with, which activities are set out for them and how they are going to set about using those activities and where they are going with them.

Bilingual and multilingual learner support

Deployment of bilingual and multilingual adult support for bilingual and multilingual pupils requires the same sensitivity and tact to be demonstrated by NQTs as is shown to any other adult. Indeed, bilingual and multilingual staff should be enabled to work in all areas of a school's programme. Bilingual and multilingual staff play a vital role in promoting learning and need to be supported in the work they do with pupils and families. Bilingualism and multilingualism present positive benefits to all, for educational, social, economic and family reasons. Indeed, the TTA and other agencies in consultation with teachers and various community groups need to urgently consider the role of Asian languages and the way the National Curriculum renders them less important than European ones.

Some practical strategies of working with bilingual and multilingual staff offered by Siraj-Blatchford and Clarke (2000) include: encouraging bilingual and multilingual staff to add to all school resources, but also to bilingual and multilingual resources, and encouraging bilingual and multilingual staff to plan group times in both languages every day. Other examples include having bilingual and multilingual signs in and around the school, translating various notices around the school and having these next to the English ones, and making sure the physical environment reflects the home languages and cultures of the pupils. Using photographs in the classroom can be a challenging and exciting activity, full of potential for language work. Involving pupils in the experience of preparing for and meeting a visitor can be a rich source of pleasure and interest and give many opportunities for language work. There should be many chances to develop skills across different language levels like casual talk, response to visual and aural stimuli, listening to and telling unscripted stories and letter-writing.

Teamworking and team building

Effective teams do not happen by chance, they have to be deliberately created and systematically managed and nurtured. As a member of a team, you need to be concerned with feelings and consciousness as well as with structures. Effective team building is facilitated by getting to know individuals, getting to know their strengths and getting to know how you can work together. All these require a free flow of information and meetings which are well organised and where there is sharing of responsibilities. Tensions arise when certain members of the team do not contribute their share equally or there is a misunderstanding of each member's roles and responsibilities. Sometimes a task explained to a member of the support staff is not made clear or s/he misunderstands what you require, leading to undue anxiety, which must be sensitively and patiently resolved.

Pupils working with teaching assistants or other adults give confidence to both and help to foster greater trust and respect by the pupils for these professionals. Shaw (2001) notes that learning support assistants feel valued when working collaboratively and find it is better for learning if there is a good team supporting a pupil or pupils. She also found that pupils feel secure if the adult team is strong, especially in presenting a united front in maintaining discipline in the class. Teamworking between teachers and support staff takes time to be established and may even require changes in the classroom structure and organisation towards more collaborative ways of working. Shaw (2001) observes that where there are open-plan sections connected to different key stages, adults and teachers are more likely to work more effectively in teams. The quality of communication between team members is crucial in order to maintain continuity for pupils. Flexibility in deploying learning support staff might be a way forward.

Schools operate partly on the basis of teams. Examples include working alongside other colleagues in a cooperative team-teaching situation. Good examples have been noted by the author where English as an additional language specialists, bilingual and multilingual teachers and instructors and SEN specialists have planned and taught some sessions. Teachers and other adults who belong to these groups are expected to act collaboratively with each other in order to meet school or team objectives. Collegiality places emphasis on teamwork where the talents of all team members can be harnessed.

Conclusions

To conclude, learning support assistants and other adults are very important people when used effectively in schools. To produce good practice, NQTs must appreciate the role of these supporters and try to encourage school managers to provide support, guidance and sound training for them. It is equally important for experienced staff to go on supporting NQTs who at times may be feeling susceptible. Lastly, as support for their school, learning support assistants and other professionals must be considered 'not just part of the staff, but are part of a team' (DfES 2002a: 3), and NQTs have a decisive role to enable this to happen for the benefit of all pupils. Improving practice when working with learning support assistants can be conducted by carrying out an audit of current practice (see DfES 2002b, Teaching Assistants' web page). So for example, teaching assistants can be trained to deliver literacy sessions as part of a whole-school Literacy initiative. When undertaken with care and sensitivity, this can develop and motivate colleagues to get better at what they are doing (DfES 2002b).

Acknowledgment

The author would like to acknowledge the very great help of Ms Malini Mistry, an experienced infant teacher, in providing a range of examples of good practice of working with NQTs, teachers and other adults.

References

Ainscow, M. (2000) 'Poor Tactics Lets Down Mums' Army', in *Times Educational Supplement* (31 March), p. 24.

Balshaw, M. (1999) *Help in the Classroom*, 2nd edn. London: David Fulton Publishers.

Bell, L. (2000) 'The Management of Staff: Some Issues of Efficiency and Cost Effectiveness', in M. Coleman and L. Anderson (eds) *Managing Finance and Resources in Education*. London: Paul Chapman Publishing.

Booth, T., Ainscow, M., Black-Hawkins, K., Vaughan, M. and Shaw, L. (2000) *Index for Inclusion*. Bristol: CSIE.

Bush, T. (1994) 'Theory and practice in educational management' in T. Bush and John West-Burnham (eds) *The Principles of Educational Management*. Harlow: Longman.

Cole, M., Hill, D. and Shan, S. (eds) (1997) *Promoting Equality in Primary Schools*. London: Cassell.

Coleman, M., Bush, T. and Glover, D. (1994) *Managing Finance and External Relations*. Harlow: Longman.

Crowther, D., Dyson, A. and Millward, A. (1998) *Costs and Outcomes for Pupils/ Students with Moderate Learning Difficulties in Special and Mainstream Schools.* Research Report RR89. London: Department for Education and Employment.

DfEE (1998) *Teachers: Meeting the Challenge of Change.* London: The Stationery Office.

DfEE (2000) *Working with Teaching Assistants, A Good Practice Guide.* London: The Stationery Office.

DfES (2002a) *14–19: Extending Opportunities, Raising Standards,* http://www.dfes. gov.uk/14-19greenpaper/foreword.shtml. Accessed 21 February 2002.

DfES (2002b) *Working with Teaching Assistants: a Good Practice Guide,* www.dfes. gov.uk/teachingreforms/support/teachassist/goodpractice/01.shtm1. Accessed 21 February 2002.

Hill, D. and Cole, M. (eds) (1999) *Promoting Equality in Secondary Schools.* London: Cassell.

Hoyle, E. (1986) *The Politics of School Management.* London: Hodder and Stoughton.

McPherson, A. (1997) 'Measuring Added Value in Schools', in A. Harris, N. Bennett and M. Preedy (eds) *Organisational Effectiveness and Improvement in Education.* Milton Keynes: Paul Chapman Publishing.

Mortimore, P., Mortimore, J. with Thomas H. (1994) *Managing Associate Staff: Innovation in Primary and Secondary Schools.* London: Paul Chapman Publishing.

Noble, R. E. (2002) 'An Analysis of the Cost Effectiveness of the Use of Support Staff at St Peter's Junior School'. Unpublished MBA assignment, University of Leicester, Educational Management Development Unit, Northampton.

OFSTED (1996) *The Education of Travelling Children – a Survey of Educational Provision for Travelling Children.* London: OFSTED.

Payne, A., Christopher, M., Clark, M. and Peck, H. (1995) *Relationship Marketing for Competitive Advantage: Winning and Keeping Customers.* Oxford: Butterworth-Heinemann.

The Runnymede Trust (1993) *Equality Assurance in Schools: Quality, Identity, Society – a Handbook for Action Planning and School Effectiveness.* Stoke-on-Trent: Trentham Books.

Scott, P. (1989) 'Accountability, Responsiveness and Responsibility', in R. Glatter (ed.) *Educational Institutions and their Environments: Managing the Boundaries.* Milton Keynes: Open University Press.

Shaw, L. (2001) *Learning Supporters and Inclusion.* Bristol: CSIE.

Siraj-Blatchford, I. and Clarke, P. (2000) *Supporting Identity, Diversity and Language in the Early Years.* Buckingham: Open University Press.

Stokes, D. (1996) 'Relationship Marketing in Primary Schools', in *Proceedings of the 'Markets in Education, Policy, Process and Practice' Symposium.* University of Southampton: Centre for Research in Education Marketing.

Sweeney, D. (1999) 'Liaising with Parents, Carers and Agencies', in M. Cole (ed.) *Professional Issues for Teachers and Student Teachers.* London: David Fulton Publishers.

Teacher Training Agency (TTA) (2002a) *Qualifying to Teach.* London: DfES.

Teacher Training Agency (TTA) (2002b) *Handbook on Guidance on QTS Standards and ITT Requirements.* London: DfES.

Tett, L., Caddell, D., Crowther, J. and O'Hara, P. (2000) *Parents and Schools: partnership in Early Years' Education,* (www.leeds.ac.uk/educol/documents/00001681.htm). Accessed 23 January 2002.

Whalley, M. (2001) *Involving Parents in their Children's Learning.* London: Paul Chapman Publishing.

CHAPTER 7

Becoming a creative teacher

Valerie Coultas

1.7 Those awarded Qualified Teacher Status must understand and uphold the professional code of the General Teaching Council for England by demonstrating that they are able to improve their own teaching, by evaluating it, learning from the effective practice of others and from evidence. They need to demonstrate that they are motivated and able to take increasing responsibility for their own professional development (TTA 2002: 6).

An effective teacher is someone who sees himself or herself as a learner. Teachers who evaluate and change their own practice to benefit their pupils and are rewarding colleagues. They make teaching a highly creative experience. Often the most useful lesson observations can be those carried out by a teacher who is your peer, someone who has to battle with the same problems you face. If you can plan lessons collaboratively, focusing on the same topic /text or the same type of pedagogy, and then evaluate these lessons together, it will help improve your practice. It is through close collaboration, shared evaluation and team teaching that teachers can make breakthroughs and deliver the most successful lessons. When team teaching, a colleague can often notice a detail in the instructions that you have missed out by closely watching the response of the pupils. Even the most experienced teachers can benefit from this process of collaboration.

It is far more positive to have these discussions with colleagues than to wait for an Inspector to point out your errors to you. If you start teaching with this view of classroom practice, you will automatically evaluate your lessons. An energetic professional teacher is self-critical and creative. Once you adopt this approach to teaching you will never lose it. This view of teachers values the voice of the teacher and sees the teacher as an agent of change within the school.

Teamwork

Many schools encourage this kind of collaboration through teamwork in departments and joint planning between teachers in different phases. The best schemes of work are often produced and evaluated collectively. Sometimes it is through a one-to-one discussion with your line manager during, for example, a feedback from a lesson observation that useful advice will be offered. Sometimes useful advice can be offered to a line manager in a support and supervision interview. Often it's the informal discussions with a colleague at break or after school that leads to a new approach in your teaching.

However, the attempt to impose quantitative targets on those discussions by the Government through performance-related pay fails to comprehend the essence of good teaching which is teamwork and intellectual collaboration. A department or a school's results are not good because of isolated, inspired individuals but because good practice is shared, knowledge and expertise are valued, and colleagues and managers give positive support and advice to staff when required. Teachers are not working on production lines in industry. They are nurturing, training, educating and developing young people. Their intellectual energy is encouraged by good advice, good leadership and shared values – not through the imposition of individual targets. The teacher is a creative professional, not a skilled technician implementing the advice of government departments.

The Government's search for quantitative, measurable data to prove success can often dismiss qualitative improvements in schools. Education cannot be reduced to the acquiring of skills; the ticking boxes agenda is reductionist. As Caroline Benn (2001) suggests, the 'limited target culture' can have the effect of losing sight of the broader aims of education and the emotional and moral aspects of learning. Fortunately many practitioners are aware of this and have attempted to set individual targets that are more holistic and relate to broader educational and training needs.

Targets for improvement

It is suggested that teachers should identify areas for their own development and set targets for improvement. It may be that this will involve closely analysing exam results at the end of a Key Stage of a group that you have taught in order to evaluate your success. It could involve an evaluation with the pupils at the end of a unit or course using their individual self-assessments. The response of the pupils themselves to a unit of work or a course is often a key indicator of successful teaching and it can help you to make adjustments to improve the content, the pedagogy or focus more closely on particular skills the pupils need.

Such an assessment, a qualitative judgement or piece of research is of particular value to you as a teacher. It shows the pupils that you value their opinions and it is useful for precise subject targets. If whole departments engage in this process it means that the course will continually improve. The process of identifying areas for development individually can therefore be assisted by an INSET session, a departmental or phase discussion led by your team leader or a line management review. But as a learning teacher you will come to those discussions with an awareness of where you have done well and how you can improve. You will even suggest themes for INSET and training to ensure that staff development serves your needs.

A teacher should also seek to improve their subject knowledge and build on areas of specialism. It is vital that teachers not only have secure knowledge of the subjects they teach but that they are aware of the new developments in those subjects, for example the new frameworks for teaching literacy and numeracy (DfEE 1998) and the debates these have generated. There are also areas of specialism within a subject that teachers may wish to become more familiar with. For example in a core subject, such as English, there are many possible subdivisions – oracy, ICT, media studies, poetry, drama, non-fiction writing and research. To gain greater expertise in one of these areas could be a goal that strengthens your teaching.

Equality and equal opportunity

In Primary and Secondary schools it may be a Key Stage or pastoral issues where you wish to specialise. An important area of knowledge the new teacher will have to develop relates to equality and equal opportunity issues. This is relevant to how you teach and how you build up relationships with pupils and colleagues. You must ensure you can identify and address all the different needs in the classroom. Lesson planning needs to address pupils with special needs, bilingual needs and high attainers. Even though setting is more common in Secondary schools, you cannot assume the same ability level in each class. You must also be aware of how to involve boys and girls in the lesson. You can ensure that boys do not dominate oral work by preparing pupils to answer questions and asking particular pupils to answer on some occasions. You can use writing frames/planning activities and clear time limits to ensure boys actually do some extended writing.

It is important that teachers have a sophisticated understanding of these issues as they are constantly alive within the classroom and you have to be aware of all the different social divisions to mediate effectively between them. This includes all forms of sexism, towards boys and girls, and the need to combat racism and homophobic bullying. You must also recognise the divisive effects of social class and counter any discrimination based on disability. You must also show by the way you use praise and how you choose pupils to help you that you value all pupils equally, regardless of race, gender, class, sexual orientation or disability. You are a role model for the pupils and they will watch what you do and compare it with what you say.

As Cole (2002: 3–4) has argued, these social divisions 'are not inevitable features of any society' but they are a product of socialisation. Children can respond in contradictory ways to these issues. Often they will challenge these divisions quite spontaneously because their socialisation is incomplete. On other occasions they will also reproduce these social divisions very crudely. Teachers can intervene in this process to educate children very effectively if they understand equality and equal opportunity issues. For a wider discussion of the breadth of these professional issues related to equality see Cole *et al.* (eds) 1997; Cole 1999; Hill and Cole (eds) 1999; Cole (ed.) 2002; and Hill and Cole (eds) 2001.

Classroom management

For many teachers new to the classroom a key area will be the issue of classroom management. This is often the primary concern of a new teacher and it is an area where they feel they have the least training. A teacher will gain a lot of good ideas by observing good practice in their own school but two useful guides with particularly practical advice on classroom management and good advice on handling challenging pupils have been written: these are Marland (1993) and Blum (1998). The latter text is useful for understanding how positive behaviour policies and praise can be used very effectively in turbulent classrooms. The new teacher would benefit from learning more about the idea of positive or assertive discipline, as it is one of the most important and practical theories that teachers have developed to handle disruptive behaviour. While it is formally subscribed to by many, the importance of rewarding good behaviour is often underestimated in practice, particularly in Secondary schools.

Since the Thatcher era there has been an increase in selection in Secondary schools. The decision to develop specialist and Faith schools in the new Green Paper will not only continue but as Hattersley (2002) argues will actually *extend* this process and dismantle the comprehensive system. This has meant that many teachers working in schools that have a more socially disadvantaged intake now face challenging behaviour in *all* their classrooms. Such schools are also under constant pressure to raise standards and compete with schools who have creamed off the less disadvantaged pupils/students where the behaviour is in general less challenging. Thrupp (2000), in an article reviewing the school improvement agenda, has listed some of the possible negative effects of this kind of pressure on such schools. In this article he argues that this 'over-optimistic view of schools improving against the odds' could mean that the school improvers fail to question the 'further polarisation of school intakes by educational quasi-markets' (p. 2). He also suggests that they 'downplay the importance of state support for disadvantaged schools by putting too much emphasis on their ability to be self-managing' (p. 2).

For the new teacher strategies to improve their classroom management skills will be a top priority, particularly in these challenging environments. All schools should have induction programmes to assist new staff and allow them time to observe other colleagues to gain knowledge of the range of strategies that can be used to address the needs of these pupils. Team teaching is also a valuable way to mentor and build confidence among new staff. I would argue that in challenging schools new staff need more time to observe and teacher tutors should be given time to really tutor.

Pedagogy

The methods that you use in the classroom are very important if you wish pupils to really learn something new each lesson. Didactic teaching methods are still relied on by large numbers of teachers, particularly in Secondary schools, but there are a lot of young learners who find this a difficult way to remember what they are told. Many teachers fear losing control or lack the preparation time that is required to plan the more interactive lessons. But all pupils need to be actively involved in the learning process to really make academic progress, particularly the pupils who are less motivated. Collaborative talk before writing is essential for bilingual and SEN pupils but it also improves the writing of all pupils. Lessons need to be planned that have an interactive element at their core (Coultas 2001). Primary school teachers can ensure this through joint planning but in Secondary schools, where teachers follow a scheme of work, staff can often avoid planning interactive lessons and rely on teacher talk or even copying large junks of text from the OHP, the blackboard or the whiteboard.

Widening styles of teaching and addressing the multicultural identity of the pupil population was an area of expertise that flourished during the lifespan of for example, the Inner London Education Authority. A London-wide authority with large numbers of advisory teachers was able to assist teachers in experimenting with collaborative and pupil-centred materials and to produce literature based on the pupils' writing. A whole host of new literature was made available to teachers and much of it is still used in schools. Professional Associations such as NATE, the National Oracy Project (1992) and training centres such as The English and Media Centre have continued to promote styles of teaching that focus on collaborative and child-centred forms of pedagogy.

The child-centred approach to teaching was an important feature of PGCE teacher education courses prior to the Thatcher era. Teacher education for Primary and Secondary teachers emphasised the importance of real talk in the classroom and the links between talking with confidence and writing with confidence. This approach recognised the alienating features of teacher talk for working-class pupils and suggested ways of establishing real dialogues between teacher and pupil – through anecdote, group work, visiting speakers, investigation, research and discovery. The National Curriculum, informed by the Cox Report (1989), gave equal status to speaking and listening alongside reading and writing.

The National Literacy Strategy has some good advice about the modelling of oral work, reading and writing. It also usefully develops the idea that every lesson needs to be literacy-aware. But there is a danger in aspects of the strategy that it could reinforce old-fashioned didactic methods of teaching English. If teachers are forced to study short, separate texts and decontextualised grammar exercises, this could become a new version of the comprehension textbooks that made some English lessons so tedious in the early sixties. Wyse and Jones (2001) point out that in Primary schools the literacy and numeracy strategies have left little opportunity for 'creative and unpredictable aspects of development such as talk' (p. 193). They are concerned that talk takes on 'a functional quality; a means by which the skills of reading and writing may be enhanced' (p. 193). They recommend that teachers of all subjects allow talk to become 'open, exploratory, tentative, questioning, insightful and collaborative' (p. 195). This approach has long been the hallmark of good teaching and learning and will continue to be a goal for the most creative teachers. To explore and experiment with different forms of pedagogy will be a vital goal for any learning teacher.

There are also some interesting new developments in this area of pedagogy in the debate surrounding Able and Gifted pupils and the present discourse on thinking skills and the different types of learner – kinaesthetic, auditory and visual learners (Eyre 1997). Kinaesthetic learners are people who learn best through movement or touch. Auditory learners learn best through sound, and visual learners store images in their brain. Some researchers such as Noble *et al.* (2001) have suggested that boys 'form a preponderance of kinaesthetic learners' (p. 100), that they are 'active and athletic', they 'learn best through doing what is being taught' (p. 100) and that 'if there is a dearth of kinaesthetic techniques' boys will fall behind 'into a vicious circle of under-achievement' (p. 101).

It is important also to think carefully about how adults can acquire new knowledge. It cannot be assumed that all teachers learn in the same way or wish to be trained in the same way. It is up to each individual to define their own needs and learning styles as graduate teachers. Some teachers, as graduates with high levels of concentration, like to be lectured and told clearly what is expected of them at a training session. Others prefer to be involved in a much more active way in new proposals and initiatives. Some staff prefer to be given documentation before a session begins. Yet others gain knowledge and expertise from colleagues in similar roles in other schools. Another way of acquiring knowledge within school is through action research projects. I have initiated several of these projects – on gender and literacy, on oracy and teaching styles – and carried out literacy audits in different schools. I recognise this as a valuable way of teachers acquiring expertise, learning more about the institution they teach in and the needs/interests of the pupils. This is an approach which operates on a grass roots, cooperative model of teaching and on a belief that schools work best when teachers are allowed to have free souls to enquire and develop good practice.

Professional development

A learning teacher must have initiative, seek out and make use of sources of professional development. As an INSET Coordinator, I assist my colleagues by passing on the relevant training information. But individual teachers can also access the National Grid for Learning, join subject associations and attend network meetings to find the relevant forms of training to address their individual needs.

It is not only participation in training that defines the self-motivated teacher. It is also the ability to evaluate and use professional development opportunities that is vitally important. The teacher who tries out new techniques quickly after the training will incorporate that knowledge and adapt it to suit their situation. Some schools encourage each individual member of staff to evaluate their training through the provision of some kind of structure – a discussion with your line manager or an evaluation form. If not, the individual should develop their own records and process of evaluation to ensure that training is used constructively. Staff who keep a professional development portfolio will find this useful when applying for promotion.

It is often surprising how much expertise exists among staff in any one school. Schools sometimes seek advice from consultants and experts from outside the school when there is not a lot of knowledge on that subject within the school. Knowing your staff and where real knowledge and expertise lies and how to use it is a feature of good management and good teachers. I have often been surprised how willing overworked and stressed staff are to share expertise and assist other colleagues for formal and informal training. As with pupils, teachers should approach other staff carefully with specific requests for assistance and always give staff a lot of notice of extra demands. This applies to assistance with all routine duties as well as INSET. It can refer to making requests of your line manager to assist you or even your head teacher. Using the expertise of those around you is therefore a key indicator of the teacher who is a learner.

Being able to respond positively to praise, advice and criticism is also a crucial feature of a good practitioner. Having taught in two very tough London boys' schools I can attest that it's hard to accept some of the abuse that can come from pupils, nor should a teacher ever try to accept any disrespectful remarks. But when a colleague or pupil makes a thoughtful criticism it's worth while stepping back and deciding whether the criticism has any truth in it. Is there anything I can improve on here? is a question you can ask yourself. Perhaps part of the criticism can be acknowledged while part of it maybe unfair. Likewise with praise – too often we are too stressed or embarrassed and fail to acknowledge praise with a confident and positive response. Yet a motivated teacher knows that we can only survive in schools with the help, support, advice and criticism of our colleagues/pupils and that it is this collective spirit and sense of purpose that makes teaching a worthwhile profession.

The teacher's role is a nurturing one towards the young. The best teachers ensure that they build good relationships with the pupils they teach in many subtle and important ways. Although a teacher has to deal with a class as a group, a successful teacher is also able to communicate with pupils as individuals. A teacher not only has to be available for one-to-one discussion with pupils but also has to interact with colleagues. To be available for and willing to assist your colleagues is an intrinsic skill required of all teachers regardless of their status or position within a school. In my experience the more challenging the behaviour of the pupils, the greater the need for teachers to share their expertise and be available for each other. Knowledge of the individual child's background can be vital to understanding behaviour and academic progress. Having led several academic teams in different schools I know how important it is that staff understand school procedures if they are to follow them accurately. Staff who ask detailed questions about how exactly a section of a scheme of work breaks down in practice or who are able to admit that they don't fully understand what their role as tutor involves, assist all new staff. This is the same with whole-school issues in staff meetings. Teachers who fail to articulate their difficulties and concerns are far less likely to be following the school and department policies so consistently as those who acknowledge their needs for help.

One of the negative features of re-structuring 'failing' schools in the 1990s was that staff were prevented from asking questions and reflecting on new policies because of the pressure of continuous inspection and the fear of being labelled troublesome. This led to many good teachers, particularly some of the most altruistic ones, changing schools, careers or even opting for early retirement and voluntary redundancy, which added to the crisis of teacher supply, a particularly severe problem now in challenging inner-city schools. It became unfashionable for teachers to talk of the realities of social deprivation and the effects in schools because this became an apology for 'low expectations'. Instead Blair's brave new world of education demanded high expectations and an end to the idea that social class determined or even influenced academic achievement. Mackie (2000) has written a very personal account of the effects of this on the lives of pupils and teachers in these schools. The reality is that social class has always played and continues to play a vital role in determining educational achievement (Hill and Cole 2001) and while all teachers must have high expectations for all, they must also have a realistic understanding of how social class affects educational achievement.

An excellent training programme I attended at Stoke Rochford suggested that all teachers should view themselves as 'managers' of the classroom and managers and leaders of others. This view of the classroom teacher is important as it emphasises the variety and breadth of knowledge and skills a teacher possesses. The teacher's role was to empower pupils and manage the classroom. As teachers we could also empower each other by the way we related to each other in schools, sharing expertise and good practice.

Collaboration

When assistance is offered to you as a teacher you should know how to use it appropriately. Having worked very closely with bilingual and SEN colleagues and learning support assistants I am very interested when they give me examples of staff who do not know how to receive and use support. If your lessons have an interactive/pair or group work element you will always provide a role for another adult as they can easily target one group or you can target a group and they can circulate. Reading aloud can always be made more enjoyable for the pupils when different adults participate. If it is planned support, teachers or support staff can read with a group or individuals or prepare a reading for the class with a particular group. Specialist staff are often willing to prepare materials for particular pupils if the classroom teacher makes the task clear. Collaboration with support staff is much easier when the support is a regular feature of a lesson each week and the relationship between the two adults has time to develop. When SEN and E2L staff are allocated to departments or year groups the collaboration is greatly improved as the support staff have a clear overview of the curriculum.

A second adult, who is there to help, is always welcome in my classroom. The very presence of another adult makes me feel more relaxed and able to be more adventurous in my teaching. There are often unusual spin-offs from lessons that are taught by two adults. Recently after a brief row with a colleague over cover I was sent a supply teacher to team-teach my lesson by way of apology. The teacher enthusiastically joined in the lesson on war poetry where the pupils were asked to draw a collage of pictures to illustrate the poem 'Dulce et Decorum Est' by Wilfred Owen in a unit on war poetry. The teacher not only joined in the reading of the poem aloud but he also drew his own sketches of the poem to the delight of the students around him. They were very good sketches. The next lesson I used those sketches on an OHP to revise the poem and take the pupils into the next exercise.

The pupils and the staff had a good feeling about that lesson. The assistance of another adult can be of great benefit to the pupils and the teacher. There is often a more democratic ethos in a classroom where the teaching is shared on a more long-term basis and more independent learning can take place. Even short-term assistance, to remove a troublesome child or quieten down a noisy group, is also sometimes required and teachers should learn to welcome that assistance and not be fearful that it diminishes their authority.

Finally the teacher who is a learner can always contribute to the development of other colleagues. Your enthusiasm for your subject or favoured forms of pedagogy may motivate both students and colleagues. Your belief in the value of teaching and education as a source for the enrichment of society can inspire others. Your belief that education can be a source for change towards building a more egalitarian society will motivate pupils and colleagues alike. Your practical advice and explanations of how to overcome difficulties and persevere will always be of value to your colleagues. As a creative teacher, you can adapt, amend, and integrate new ideas about teaching. New teachers, fresh from university, can enrich schools by looking at them with new eyes, and can contribute new ideas, approaches and insights. As teachers and learners, our minds should never be closed to learning something new.

References

Benn, C. (2001) 'A Credible Alternative: Some Tasks for the Future', *Education and Social Justice*, 3(2), (Autumn).

Blum, P. (1998) *Succeeding and Surviving in Difficult Classrooms.* London: Routeledge.

Cole, M. (1999) 'Professional issues and Initial Teacher Education: what can be done and what could be done', *Education and Social Justice*, 2(1), 63–6.

Cole, M. (2002) 'Introduction: Human Rights, Education and Equality', in M. Cole (ed.) *Education, Equality and Human Rights: Issues of Gender, 'Race', Sexuality, Special Needs and Social Class*. London: Routledge/Falmer.

Cole, M. (ed.) (2002) *Education, Equality and Human Rights: Issues of Gender, 'Race', Sexuality, Special Needs and Social Class*. London: Routledge/Falmer.

Cole, M., Hill, D. and Shan, S. (eds) (1997) *Promoting Equality in Primary Schools*. London: Cassell.

Coultas, V. (2001) Oracy Across the Curriculum: Selhurst High School. Unpublished paper.

Cox Report. Department of Education and Science and The Welsh Office (1989) *English for Ages 5–16* (The Second Cox Report). York: National Curriculum Council.

Department for Education and Employment (DfEE) (1998) *The National Literacy Strategy – Framework for Teaching*. London: DfEE.

Eyre, D. (1997) *Able Children in Ordinary Schools*. London: David Fulton Publishers.

Hattersley, R. (2002) 'Education, Education, Education: A Commitment Reviewed', *Education and Social Justice*, 4(1), 2–6 (Winter).

Hill, D. and Cole, M. (eds) (1999) *Promoting Equality in Secondary Schools*. London: Cassell.

Hill, D. and Cole, M. (2001) 'Social Class', in D. Hill and M. Cole (eds) (2001) *Schooling and Equality: Fact, Concept and Policy*. London:Kogan Page.

Hill, D. and Cole, M. (eds) (2001) *Schooling and Equality: Fact, Concept and Policy*. London: Kogan Page.

Mackie, J. (2000) 'The Death of the Inner London Comprehensive', *Education and Social Justice*, 2(3), 2–5 (Summer).

Marland, M. (1975) *The Craft of the Classroom: A Survival Guide*. Oxford: Heinemann Educational.

National Oracy Project (1992) *Thinking Voices: The Work of the National Oracy Project*. London: Hodder and Stoughton.

Noble, C., Brown, J. and Murphy, J. (2001) *How to Raise Boys' Achievement*. London: David Fulton Publishers.

Teacher Training Agency (TTA) (2002) *Qualifying to Teach*. London: DfES.

Thrupp, M. (2000) 'Compensating for Class: Are School Improvement Researchers Being Realistic?', *Education and Social Justice*, 2(2), (Spring).

Wyse, D. and Jones, R. (2001) *Teaching English, Language and Literacy*. London: Routledge/Falmer.

CHAPTER 8

Schoolteachers' conditions of service

Jeff Nixon

Introduction

What do we mean by conditions of service? In the 1920s and 1930s for example, a woman teacher could be dismissed if she got married or even kept company with men. She was not allowed to ride in a carriage or automobile with any man except her brother or father. She had to be home between the hours of 8 p.m. and 6 a.m., unless in attendance at a school function, and could not leave town without first obtaining the permission of the Board of Trustees. The contract also laid down a non-negotiable dress code which included the prohibition of make-up and stipulated that she should not be seen in places such as ice-cream stores (Teacher's Contract 1923: *Women In Education*).

Eighty years later, for those teachers employed in LEA-maintained schools, national conditions of service are derived from two basic sources. The first is the *Schoolteachers' Pay and Conditions Document* (DfES 2002a), often referred to as the 'Blue Book'. This sets out working time, professional duties and conditions of service. The second is *Conditions of Service for Schoolteachers in England and Wales* (Council of Local Education Authorities/Schoolteacher Committee (CLEA/ST), revised edn, August, 2000) (the 'Burgundy Book'). This covers national agreements between local education authorities and the teachers' organisations, including such issues as sick pay, sick leave, maternity pay and periods of notice.

Much of what happens in schools is, however, subject to local interpretation. In addition, initiatives may occur either at local or national level which change certain aspects of the teacher's job or may simply emphasise one or a number of items in the conditions of service package at a particular time; for example, the administration in different schools of in-service education and training days (INSET) – the so-called 'Baker Days'. These are named after Kenneth Baker who, as Secretary of State for Education and Science, introduced them in the Teachers' Pay and Conditions Act of 1987. The Act does not specify where or when the INSET days need to be taken, so some schools have operated sessions known as 'twilight training', whereby INSET is carried out during the school's academic year. This is often with the agreement of the staff concerned, with some schools converting days designated as 'Baker Days' into days of school closure. However, if this is the case the school must provide the statutory 190 days of education for all pupils. Teachers are required to be available for work in school for 195 days in any school year, although during the Golden Jubilee Year in 2002 this was reduced by one day for both pupils and teachers.

There may also be local agreements, on issues not covered elsewhere. These may be better or worse than conditions agreed nationally. On the positive side, for example, some LEAs operate a maternity leave and maternity pay agreement that is better than the national one. On the negative side, there exist in the aided or voluntary sector and now in Foundation Schools – formerly Grant Maintained Schools (where the governing body is the employer of teachers) – conditions of service which may not be in teachers' best interests. In Church schools, for example, it is not uncommon to see a clause in the contract of employment that states that the employee should not engage in any activity that may bring the Church into disrepute. This is frequently subject to interpretation at local level within the parish. Here one can see shades of the 1920s contract, with teachers in such schools rarely realising the position they are in until the local parish notable starts asking questions.

All this paints rather a confusing picture. Many teachers enter the profession believing, like many members of the public, that there is in existence a national system of education that is consistent across the country. This is simply not the case. When one adds the differences that exist in sixth-form colleges (independent employers since 1993), City Technology Colleges and the independent sector, and the variations in Scotland and Northern Ireland, the picture becomes even more confused. There are at least four major threats to unified pay and conditions of service arrangements. The first is the introduction of performance-related pay.

The second is the creation of Education Action Zones (EAZs). EAZs were able to 'opt out' of national agreements. However, in practice, none of the EAZs did opt out of the national arrangements on pay for teachers; the threat that the EAZs posed on this issue clearly diminishes as the zones come to an end, having served their usefulness politically (for a critique of EAZs, see, for example, Cole 1998 and Hatcher 1998).

The third is the creation of 'advanced skills teachers' (see DfES 2002a, in Appendix 1 at the end of this chapter). Each AST shall be paid on a range of any five consecutive points on the pay spine, which ranges from £28,950 to £46,164 (as at April 2002) with movement up that particular individual range determined by performance which must be a sustained high standard (DfES 2002a: 31). The Press labelled this new grade 'super teacher' and highlighted a potential earning power of £46,000+ per annum. It is unclear where the Advanced Skills Teacher (AST) will fit into the normal management structure of schools, and the proposed salary levels will adversely affect the already poor levels of recruitment, particularly in primary schools, to vacancies for headships and deputy headships. The idea that this grade will recruit high-flying graduates into the teaching profession is particularly debatable; graduates will assess the likelihood of progressing to the higher salary levels against the salaries currently available in other professions and other sectors of the economy (see Appendix 1).

Schools are dependent on a well-qualified, highly motivated team of staff working together. The AST grade is potentially a divisive and damaging imposition on the education service that will certainly have repercussions in both the short and long terms. It would appear that Government has not clearly thought through this controversial strategy in relation to the overall benefits to the education of pupils; in particular, its stated aim of improving standards.

The National Union of Teachers urged the Government to establish a working party to examine in detail the introduction of the AST grade, but to no avail. Consequently, its General Secretary, Doug McAvoy, wrote to all the other teaching unions and associations, all the LEAs and bodies representing school governors to urge such a working party to oversee the introducion of ASTs. The debate on this issue will thus continue.

Another potentially divisive element within the system is the introduction of Beacon Schools. Since April 1998, the extra money for Beacon School status would amount to a maximum of £50,000 per school to cover the extra work arising from the liaison necessary with other schools. The first group of such schools started in the Autumn of 1998 and were selected from the 159 schools named in Her Majesty's Chief Inspector of Schools Annual Report for 1996/97 as 'best performing' schools. Initially, Beacon School status lasts for three years.

As the General Secretary of the NUT, Doug McAvoy, suggested in a press release about the Beacon Schools announcement, the 100 named schools did not represent the sum total of successful schools; those on the list just happened to be there by chance as having recently been inspected and meeting the particular criteria of success on the day. McAvoy went on to say that it was not acceptable to assume these Beacon Schools are better than those which have not had the opportunity to be included in the Oscar-style winners list. He did accept, however, that schools which possess valuable expertise should be expected to share practical support and advice with other schools; such an approach he welcomed and certainly the improved funding to underpin the development should not be criticised.

Since September 2000, teachers who reach the top of the main pay scale became eligible to cross the threshold on to the Upper Pay Scale (£27,894 to £32,250 as at April 2002). This involves eligible teachers completing a form covering the following areas of their work:

- Knowledge and Understanding
- Teaching and Assessment
- Pupil Progress
- Wider Professional Effectiveness
- Professional Characteristics (see Appendix 2 at the end of this chapter).

The information on the forms is assessed first by the head teacher, then a sample are validated by an external adviser provided by Cambridge Educational Associates (CEA)(a private company, providing a range of educational and personnel services to LEAs and schools). Those teachers who are not successful during this first phase can ask for a review of the decision and CEA provides Review Officers to carry out this process.

The vast majority of teachers who applied have been successful in receiving the £2,001 extra salary. The money to provide schools with the ability to pay these increases came in the main from the Government's Standards Fund (a DfES centrally held fund to cover a wide range of LEA and school initiatives, including the funding of pay increases for teachers, head teachers and deputy head teachers). However, progression up the Upper Pay Scale will not now be funded so generously and the Secretary of State for Education and Skills, Estelle Morris, has said that she believes there is enough money in schools' budgets to pay for those teachers who progress to point 2 on the Upper Pay Scale from September 2002.

A potential dispute over the funding of this progression up the Upper Pay Scale was avoided with an agreement being reached between Estelle Morris and the leaders of the NAHT (National Association of Headteachers) and SHA (Secondary Heads Association) in early April 2002. Whilst avoiding a dispute, the agreement failed to find favour with the NUT and the NASUWT; there could easily be further problems on this issue at a later date.

The 'Blue Book': Schoolteachers' Pay and Conditions Document (STPACD) in England and Wales

The genesis of the 'Blue Book' can be found in the national salaries and conditions of service dispute, of 1986–87 (NUT 1987). While the dispute was going on, important discussions and negotiations on conditions of service took place under the auspices of the Advisory, Conciliation and Arbitration Service (ACAS). These included class size and hours worked in relation to duties and responsibilities. Up to this time there had been no guidance to quantify the amount of time teachers should spend on the range of professional duties in which they were engaged. Indeed the only reference to the teachers' day, duties and holiday entitlement was contained in the second edition of the 'Burgundy Book', paragraph 11, which simply stated, 'there are no existing national collective agreements on these matters beyond that affecting the school mid-day break' (CLEA/ST 1985: 11).

The Teachers' Pay and Conditions Act of 1987, one of the shortest pieces of legislation on the statute book, required the Secretary of State to appoint an Interim Advisory Committee to examine and report on matters referred to it concerning pay and other conditions of employment of teachers in England and Wales. It also empowered the Secretary of State to make orders covering these matters. Before making such orders, the Secretary of State is required to consult with appointed representatives of the LEAs, governors of voluntary schools and schoolteachers. The

STPACD has been produced annually and is preceded by a lengthy consultation exercise during which the teacher unions are able to make either joint or separate submissions to a Review Body, set up under the Teachers' Pay and Conditions Act of 1991. Normally, any joint submission is coordinated by the National Union of Teachers and time is allocated for the presentation of oral evidence. This provides the General Secretaries of the Unions and Associations the opportunity to address the Review Body directly.

Prior to this system being introduced, *negotiations* on pay and conditions of service took place in the Burnham Committee and the CLEA/ST, respectively. The Burnham Committee was abolished under the provision of the Teachers' Pay and Conditions Act 1987, whereas CLEA/ST still exists but rarely meets. An Order which provided for conditions of employment to be incorporated into teachers' contracts also came into force in 1987. The National Union of Teachers took no part in the consultations, arguing instead that until the Secretary of State was prepared to discuss the restoration of teachers' negotiating rights, any consultations would simply be a cosmetic exercise.

The conditions of service elements of the Order dealt with teachers' duties and working time only. They contained little safeguard against the excessive workload which was being imposed upon teachers. The Order set down a contractual requirement that teachers should be available for work on 195 days per year of which 190 days would be spent with pupils. It also specified a list of required professional duties (the 2002 list is reproduced in Appendix 3 to this chapter). These cover teaching, related activities, assessments and reports, appraisal, review of further training and development, educational methods, discipline, health and safety, staff meetings, cover for absent teachers, public examinations, management and administration.

In 2001, there was an important development in relation to the amount of cover an individual teacher would be expected to provide. Within the STPACD, there are caveats within the sections on teachers providing cover that are not particularly helpful in placing a limitation on the amount of cover for absence teachers do. In effect, teachers could be required to cover on an unlimited basis if the management within the school maintained it was not possible to find supply teachers to do the work.

Following a dispute over this element of teachers' professional duties, a National Agreement on cover was negotiated. This provided for teachers to cover beyond the three days of an unexpected absence or beyond the two days of an anticipated absence if the school could not find supply staff to employ. However, the teachers who provide the cover are allowed to 'bank' the time and be given it back as non-contact time, or indeed free time, at a later point. This is a very important development and means that the working time elements of the 'Blue Book' can no longer be applied as strictly as they have been.

The final section entitled 'Administration' contains an important requirement that is worth examining in more detail. The phrase in question implies a responsibility for 'supervising pupils . . . before, during or after school sessions'. The question of responsibility for pupils before, during and after school session times is an important point and needs clarification. Schools, and head teachers in particular, should make it clear to parents/carers that the supervision of pupils by the school begins and ends at particular times. Many parents/carers may be in the habit of dropping children off at school some time before school begins. The NUT recommends to heads and members that teachers are available to receive pupils ten minutes before the start of the school day and to dismiss them up to ten minutes after the school day ends. Between morning and afternoon sessions, the Union recommends that members are available for five minutes beyond the morning session to supervise pupils going to lunch either on or off the school premises and are available to receive pupils once more five minutes before the start of the afternoon session. It is important that this time forms part of the directed-time element of teachers' professional duties in case an accident occurs. If head teachers include this in the allocation of 1,265 hours of directed time for the year, it would amount to 95 hours of directed time for all teachers in the school year. It may be possible, however, in larger schools to organise this responsibility on a rota basis. Heads should also let parents/carers know in writing that these are the arrangements and that the school can only accept responsibility for the supervision of pupils at particular stated times.

Apart from the obvious concerns about pupil welfare and safety, there are legal implications. *Barnes v Hampshire County Council* (Local Government Review 1969) concerned a five-year-old girl who, in 1962, left school before the end of the school day which was known as 3.30 p.m. The girl should have been met at the school gate by her mother. However, on this particular day, the mother had not yet arrived. The children had been told that if no one was there to collect them, then they should return to their teacher. In this case, the girl did not do so and attempted to cross the busy A30 trunk road at a point 250 yards from the school gate. Unfortunately she was involved in an accident which resulted in serious injuries, including partial paralysis of her left arm and foot. A witness heard the accident happen and telephoned for an ambulance. His emergency call was recorded at the telephone exchange at 3.30 p.m.

Initially the parents' claim for negligence on behalf of their daughter was rejected. However, following a further rejection in the Court of Appeal, the Master of the Rolls, Lord Denning, dissented in the majority judgment and maintained that the school's system depended on the parents being there to meet the children at half past three, and on the school not letting them out until that time. To let them out before their parents were due to arrive was to release them into a situation of potential danger, and in his view this constituted a breach of duty. Previously, the judges had said that ordinary people in ordinary life do not carry a chronometer; they did not believe that three to five minutes in the case before them constituted a breach of duty.

The case was referred to the House of Lords who reversed the judgment of the Court of Appeal and awarded damages of £10,000 against the LEA. The Lords agreed with the Master of the Rolls, emphasising that it was the duty of the school authorities not to release the children before the end of the school day. While early release would seldom lead to an accident, foreseeably it could do and in this case it did.

It is important to note that, as the employer, it was the LEA which was taken to task in the above example. LEAs have a vicarious liability for the acts or omissions of employees, who are acting in the course of their employment. In these circumstances, LEAs are responsible for the payment of any award of damages or compensation. Under health and safety legislation, it is, however, possible for teachers to be fined, as was a science teacher in 1986. This teacher was fined £500 after the Health and Safety Executive brought a successful case, following investigation of an explosion during a school experiment which resulted in 15 children being taken to hospital. It was believed to be the first prosecution of a teacher under the Health and Safety at Work Act 1974.

Magistrates were told that no safety precautions were taken in the experiment for a class of twelve- and thirteen-year-olds, who were showered with sulphuric acid. Fortunately no one was seriously hurt. The teacher admitted failing to take reasonable care to protect children who were in the lesson. The magistrate told the teacher that the consequences could have been disastrous for some, if not all, the children in the class. Parents were entitled to feel their children were safe while at school. The court heard that the pupils were sprayed with acid after a flask exploded in an experiment to demonstrate the reduction of metal oxide. Although plastic screens and protective spectacles were available at the school, the teacher did not use them. The Health and Safety Inspector reported that many of the children received burns from droplets of acid on their arms and bodies. One of the children was cut by flying glass and the face of one child was only a foot away from the bottle containing the acid. Fourteen of the children taken to hospital were discharged after treatment; one stayed in hospital overnight.

The Health and Safety Inspector said there was no wish to restrict the teaching of science by banning all experiments where there was an element of risk. The inspector believed that potentially dangerous experiments could be done safely, if reasonable precautions were taken. The teacher concerned received a reprimand.

Conditions of service were changed considerably by the Education Reform Act of 1988. This provided for local management of schools (LMS), giving governing bodies much more control and seriously eroding the power of the head teacher and the LEAs. The Act also made provisions for schools to opt out of LEA control and become grant-maintained. This has subsequently been amended within the Schools Standards and Framework Act (1998), so that former GM schools are now back under the umbrella of the LEA although as most are Foundation Schools, the governors are still the employer. The overall effect was to loosen the influence LEAs had on schools and consequently potentially worsen the conditions of service of teachers at local level.

The 'Burgundy Book': Conditions of Service for Schoolteachers in England and Wales

The 'Burgundy Book' deals with sick pay and sick leave, maternity pay and maternity leave and notice. It also refers to legislation affecting teachers' conditions of service with respect to redundancy payments, unfair dismissal, sex discrimination, trade union membership and activities, time off work, race relations, health and safety at work, premature retirement and medical fitness to teach (including those medical conditions when teachers would be suspended from teaching duties on the grounds of ill-health).

Three other sections of the 'Burgundy Book' are also worthy of note. These are the model procedure to resolve collective disputes, facilities for trade union representatives and the 1968 School Meals Agreement. This agreement was a major breakthrough for teachers in that it allowed teachers the freedom to take a lunch break away from the children and the school. Teachers could no longer be required to undertake supervision at lunch time and that aspect of the conditions of service package remains intact to the present day. There is not much employment law beneficial to the workforce that has survived over 30 years. The 1968 School Meals Agreement was thus an historic landmark for teachers and, in my view, remains so.

Sick pay and sick leave

Teachers' sick pay and sick leave are detailed on a sliding scale entitlement according to length of service. During the first year of service, full pay for 25 working days is granted and, after completion of four calendar months, half pay for 50 working days. This becomes full pay for 50 working days, followed by half pay for 50 working days during the second year and full pay for 75 working days and half pay for 75 working days, during the third year. In the fourth and successive years of service, full pay for 100 working days and half pay for 100 working days is allowed. The scale is described as a minimum; some LEAs have agreed local improvements. LEAs and governing bodies will have the discretion to extend the scheme in particular circumstances although it has to be acknowledged that the introduction of LMS has made that more problematic. It must also be noted that the scale is expressed in terms of working days which means that holiday periods are discounted. However, teachers' pay continues in a holiday period at the rate it was prior to the holiday commencing; this means in fact that the actual time teachers can be on sick leave on full pay is approximately six months when in the fourth or subsequent year of service, followed by six months on half pay.

Teachers are also entitled to Statutory Sick Pay (SSP), a basic entitlement for all employees whatever their job. This is paid for the first 28 weeks of absence, after which State Incapacity Benefit must be claimed from the Department of Social Security. When a teacher is receiving full sick pay, SSP is included in this. When a teacher goes on to half pay, SSP will be paid on top. Teachers in their first year of service who have only a limited entitlement under the scheme will continue to receive SSP after their entitlement to full and half pay has run out.

Maternity leave and maternity pay

Right to maternity leave and pay are dependent upon length of service although all women teachers are entitled to a minimum of 18 weeks' maternity leave, regardless of length of service. Women teachers with at least one year's continuous service with one or more LEA by the eleventh week prior to the expected date of birth are entitled to an extended period of leave of up to 40 weeks. Normally leave before the birth of up to 11 weeks can be taken with 29 weeks of post-natal leave available. Women teachers can work closer to the expected date of the birth should they choose to do so, but they cannot add to the 29 weeks of post-natal leave any of the 11 weeks of pre-natal leave available to them but not taken as leave. Maternity pay is provided on the following basis for the duration of the maternity leave: for the first four weeks of absence, full pay; for the next two weeks 90 per cent of a week's salary, and for the remainder of the 18-week period of absence, half pay. For any remaining period of absence up to the date of return, the woman teacher receives no pay. Women teachers become eligible to receive Statutory Maternity Pay (SMP) in the period after the first six weeks of maternity pay; however, it is only paid for 18 weeks and the first six weeks are taken into account in the entitlement calculation. The current rate (April 2002) is £62.20 per week.

A woman teacher has the right to return to her job following the ending of her maternity leave although the employer may, by giving notice in writing, postpone her return by no more than four weeks after the notified date of return. The notice must specify the reason for postponement. The woman teacher must return to her job for at least 13 weeks, which effectively means at least a full term; if she does not comply with this provision she must refund some or all of her maternity pay. This requirement to return for 13 weeks may be reduced at the discretion of the employer. Frequently women teachers choose to reduce the number of hours they work upon return to work following maternity leave. Whilst there is no right to do this under the terms of the 'Burgundy Book', there are examples which can be quoted from Employment Tribunal decisions that are particularly helpful when women teachers wish to reduce their hours or change from full-time to part-time employment, or to work on a job-share basis. A refusal by employers to accept a request for a reduction of hours or to operate a job-share could give rise to a claim of sex discrimination. This happened with respect to a refusal of job-share by the Governing body of Ellis Guildford Comprehensive School and Nottinghamshire County Council. In March 1996, the Nottingham tribunal agreed that the teacher concerned had been indirectly discriminated against on grounds of her sex because she was refused a request for a job-share following maternity leave. The governors of the school attempted to argue that a job-share would create inconvenience for the school. The tribunal, however, did not accept this as a justifiable reason for refusing to arrange a job-share. It found that a requirement imposed on a woman teacher to work full-time was 'unanswerable' and amounted to indirect sex discrimination. This and the related case of *Mrs Clay v English Martyrs School* are considered to be significant decisions that give weight to requests for reduced hours or job-share, when returning to work after maternity leave.

The 'Burgundy Book' is silent on the right to paternity leave. Some LEAs, however, do include it as part of local conditions and agreements, and the NUT has campaigned for its inclusion as part of a package of measures designed to improve the conditions of service of all teachers. As an example of good practice, the NUT as an employer of staff grants ten working days for paternity leave.

However, since the introduction of Parental Leave, contained within the Employment Relations Act 1999, there is an entitlement for unpaid leave. Parents seeking this leave must have been in employment for 12 months or more and the leave is available for children born on or after 15 December 1999, or those born before that date but adopted after it. The leave can be taken any time up to and including the child's fifth birthday, taking a maximum of four weeks per child in one year. The overall maximum is 13 weeks in total from the child's birth to the fifth birthday. This parental leave does not affect the maternity leave outlined above.

Grievance, disciplinary and capability procedures

The 'Burgundy Book' places an obligation on employers (LEAs and governing bodies in relation to Foundation schools, Voluntary Aided schools, sixth-form colleges and City Technology Colleges and schools in the independent sector) to provide teachers with copies of procedures governing the resolution of grievances and discipline. Since LMS, governing bodies have usually adopted procedures recommended by the personnel sections of LEAs. It can be argued that all such procedures form part of a teacher's contract of employment and if they are not followed, this could readily give rise to a claim for breach of contract.

As far as teacher capability is concerned, an Occasional Paper written by Dr Caroline Wragg's team at the University of Exeter Teacher Competence Project (Wragg *et al.*, 1998) reported interviews conducted with teacher association/union officers which examined the manner in which capability procedures are used by schools and LEAs. The Union officers interviewed agreed that it was their job to ensure that teachers were treated fairly and properly when such procedures were used and that this should include realistic timescales in order for the teacher to be given adequate support, guidance and encouragement to improve on performance. The four-week fast track approach encouraged by the Minister for Schools, and taken up in the media, gave the public and, to some extent the profession, two false impressions: first that there are too many incompetent teachers, and second, that the Government is doing something about it.

The amendments encouraged by the Government and the DfEE covered one paragraph containing two sentences. Most LEA-recommended procedures on capability provide as many as six pages of guidance to head teachers and governors on how to apply such procedures.

Periods of notice

Normally, unless the contract of employment states differently, there are only three dates in the year when teachers can leave a job or be dismissed (except in the case of summary dismissal which can occur at any time and is usually linked to offences that can be described as gross misconduct). The dates are 31 December in the Autumn term, 30 April in the Spring term and 31 August in the Summer term. Notice must be given by the teacher or the employer on 31 October in the Autumn term, 28 or 29 February in the Spring term and 31 May in the Summer term. If a teacher leaves at the end of the Spring term and has another job to go to that starts at the end of the Easter holiday period, then salary is only paid until the day before the new job commences. However, if the teacher is not going on to work for another employer, salary is paid until 30 April. This is regardless of when Easter falls in that particular year.

If a teacher misses the notice date, the LEA or school may insist that the teacher stays until the end of the following term. In these circumstances, a teacher may apply to the head teacher and/or the Governing body of the school for what is termed 'early release' from contractual obligations. Notice periods for Foundation schools and sixth-form colleges are usually the same. In the independent sector, a full term's notice may be required in some contracts of employment and in City Technology Colleges there are variations to the 'Burgundy Book' notice periods which frequently mean teachers are under a shorter notice period.

All employees acquire rights to more notice as the period of continuous employment increases over the years. The maximum is 12 weeks' notice once the period of employment is 12 years or more and the minimum is one week. Thereafter, employees accrue an extra week's notice for every completed year of continuous service. This means that should the employer wish to give notice to terminate the contract and the teacher has, say, ten years' service, then the period of notice has to be ten weeks, under the provisions of the Employment Rights Act 1996. This provision only operates if it is the employer giving notice; it does not affect the period of notice the teacher has to give in order to leave the job. The statutory notice period can run concurrently with the notice given according to 'Burgundy Book' requirements (see previous paragraph).

Some contracts, particularly those issued to cover maternity leave or long-term absence due to illness, contain a much shorter notice period, usually one week. This is to enable the employer to comply with the rights of the employee who wishes to return to work. For women teachers who are returning to work from maternity leave this is to enable the school and the employer to comply with the 'Burgundy Book' provisions on maternity leave discussed earlier. Similarly, unless there is some doubt about a teacher's fitness to return to work following illness (and in cases where there is doubt, the employer's medical officer or occupational health advisers will be consulted), a teacher who is declared fit to return to work following illness clearly has the right to do so. This obviously has an effect on the contract given to any teacher who covers a long-term sickness absence. That is why the notice period may be as short as one week in such contracts.

Local agreements

The third component of the conditions of service package for teachers is contained within whatever local agreements have been negotiated within the LEA or the school (e.g. Foundation, Voluntary Aided or sixth-form college; it is unlikely that negotiated local agreements will exist in the independent sector as recognition of the teaching unions and associations is likely to be problematic). However, since the introduction of the right for unions to be recognised under certain specific circumstances, there have been a few instances of union recognition developing in the independent sector. Local agreements normally cover matters not covered in the 'Burgundy Book', such as time off other than for sickness and maternity leave. Entitlements or guidance to head teachers and governing bodies in exercising discretion on leave of absence covering bereavement, a relative's illness, weddings, study leave, moving house and other circumstances are all dependent on local agreements. There will not always be a right to time off for these matters and it may not always be paid leave. The decision on leave of absence may be delegated to the head teacher. This has particularly been the case since the introduction of LMS. However, the ultimate decision on the right to leave of absence will rest with the employer, which in most cases will be the LEA.

If, in an LEA school, the head teacher refuses time off for duties and/or activity related to a teacher's role as a trade union representative, the LEA may decide to intervene and advise the head to sanction the request. There is a Code of Practice produced by the Advisory, Conciliation and Arbitration Service (ACAS) (1998) that emphasises leave for such matters should not be unreasonably refused.

Other aspects of teachers' conditions of service that are determined locally are the precise timings of the school day. There are considerable variations between the Key Stages. The amount of contact time in an infant school, for example, may be around five hours, whereas in a secondary school it may be up to 5 hours 45 minutes. It is left to the school to decide the precise timings of the day, the timing of breaks, the length of morning and afternoon sessions and the length of the lunch time. Thus, some schools may operate a very short lunch break of 30 minutes whereas others, mostly primary schools, will allocate one and a half hours. The reason for such a lengthy lunch break will probably be historical and date back to the time when so many children took a school lunch that the school found it necessary to offer more than one sitting because of the size of the school hall and the limited kitchen facilities.

Circular 7/90 (DES 1990) provides a framework to manage any proposed changes and gives illustrations of average timings in different types of school. Changes to the school day can only be introduced in September of the school year and parents, the LEAs and other groups with an interest (for example, bus companies and taxi firms) need to be consulted and to be given at least three months' notice. It is interesting to note that there is no requirement in the circular to consult teachers. However, since the introduction of the Session Times (England) Regulations in 1999, any governing body wishing to make changes to the time of school sessions must consult the LEA, the head teacher and all teaching and non-teaching staff employed in the school before making the changes.

Contracts of employment

Once a job has been offered and that offer has been accepted, then a legal contract comes into existence, even if there is nothing in writing to confirm the agreement. Head teachers, governing bodies and LEAs are understandably unsympathetic to teachers agreeing to accept a post and then changing their minds (often signalling by implication that something better has been found). The redress of the school, governing body and/or LEA might take a number of different forms. They may threaten to sue the teacher concerned for breach of contract. This is technically possible although unlikely in reality. What is more likely is that expenses for attendance at the interview will not be paid. Some LEAs may take a further step of circulating the name(s) of candidates who cause this sort of inconvenience to schools in the LEA although that practice has lessened since LMS was implemented and governing bodies have much more control over the appointments procedure. Certainly it is not unusual, in the case of student teachers letting down a school or an LEA, for the training institution to be contacted and told about the student who has accepted the offer of a post and then declined it at a later stage.

There are three different types of contract: permanent[1], temporary and fixed-term. A temporary contract does not have within it a termination date; sometimes schools and LEAs will issue temporary contracts to teachers, using the phrase 'in the first instance' to suggest that at some point the contract will be made permanent. A teacher on a temporary contract would acquire employment protection rights after one year's service. Therefore, unless the temporary contract is for a genuinely temporary reason (see below), the employer should be persuaded to transfer the teacher to a permanent contract. Having said that, there have been cases where teachers have experienced year-on-year temporary contracts for as many as twelve years. Such a long period on temporary contracts almost redefines the word temporary, and is something which trade unions are constantly challenging.

A fixed-term contract is for a defined period and contains a date on which the job will end – normally the three end-of-term dates referred to in the section on notice periods: 31 December, 30 April and 31 August. Teachers who are offered fixed-term contracts should ask why it is only for a defined period (the same questions should be asked when temporary contracts are offered). Sometimes the justification given is 'for budgetary reasons', and many schools will offer such contracts on a year-by-year basis. However, what such contracts amount to is pre-selection for redundancy and they have the effect of creating two separate groups within a school:

those who are directly at risk of being declared redundant (those on temporary contracts) and the rest of the staff (on permanent or ongoing contracts) who are clearly protected from any initial selection process for redundancy.

The trade unions take the view that fixed-term or temporary contracts should only be used where there is a genuine fixed-term or temporary need which is seen from the outset to be the case. Examples would be contracts that are issued to cover a maternity leave, long-term sickness, secondment of a teacher or where a school needs to cover a vacancy while awaiting the release of a teacher from another contract. These examples will be considered legitimate uses of fixed-term or temporary contracts. It has been noticeable in recent years, certainly following the introduction of LMS and after Kenneth Clarke as Secretary of State for Education abolished the arrangements for the probationary year, that schools have been using fixed-term and temporary contracts as a device to assess a teacher's suitability for the post. This is an abuse of such contracts and it should not be used to replace a properly resourced induction period for teachers, particularly for newly qualified teachers (NQTs). Induction was introduced by the DfEE in the Teaching and Higher Education Act 1998, and it proposed to implement the relevant provisions with effect from September 1999. Since the introduction of the induction year for NQTs, the number of student teachers being offered temporary or fixed-term contracts has reduced significantly.

Another worrying aspect that emerged from research on temporary and fixed-term contracts (NUT 1995) is the number of part-time staff on such contracts. Some employers wrongly equate part-time work with temporary contracts. The majority of part-time teachers are women, and issuing only temporary part-time contracts to them as a matter of policy would be regarded as indirect sex discrimination and could give rise to an Employment Tribunal claim, without any requirement for a continuous service qualifying period. Part-time teachers should also watch out for a variable hours clause in their contracts. This clause is sometimes inserted in an attempt to manage the needs of a school from year to year. In much the same way as full-time contracts may be issued on a fixed-term or temporary basis for 'budgeting reasons', part-time contracts with a variable hours clause may well be used in a similar manner although the variable hours clause disguises that fact. Obviously there are financial implications for teachers who may have their hours of work varied from one year to another or even one term to another; if the hours are reduced the salary reduces as well. Unless the contract specifically deals with the extent of the variation, a part-time teacher could be offered work amounting to 99 per cent in one year (this is effectively full-time apart from 15 minutes in the week) and this could reduce to as little as 10 per cent the following year (one morning or afternoon per week). The effect on salary would be dramatic. In order to offset such drastic variations, some LEAs have built ranges of hours into the contracts in order to attempt to guarantee a minimum number of hours per week and consequently make the part-time teacher more financially secure.

Since the introduction of the Employment Relations Act in 1998, the use of waiver clauses in relation to unfair dismissal has been deemed unlawful. However, waiver clauses relating to redundancy payments, for which employees become eligible after two years' service with an employer, are still considered lawful. The use of such clauses again divides the workforce, separating those with employment rights from those who will never acquire such rights. Since employees have very few rights in the first place, to be asked or required to sign away these limited rights is totally unacceptable. The introduction of General Teaching Councils (GTCs) (see Chapter 9) will at least oversee abuses of contract law on behalf of the teaching profession, and may even adopt a naming and shaming policy where LEAs and schools attempting to use waiver clauses are identified.

There is one final point to make on contracts. The non-renewal of a fixed-term or temporary contract is, in the eyes of the law, a dismissal. In order to comply with the law, in carrying out the dismissal, the employer should ensure it is done fairly by applying a proper procedure to the process of dismissal. This may mean offering the opportunity to a teacher threatened with dismissal by reason of the non-renewal of a contract to make representations to the governing body or the LEA before notice of non-renewal is given. In addition, an opportunity to appeal against a recommendation to dismiss must be provided. In the maintained sector the appeal hearing must be held prior to the date on which the teacher is given notice; however, in the sixth-form sector the appeal can be heard in the notice period but obviously before the date of dismissal. If a teacher is facing the loss of a job and simply forgoes rights to a hearing, perhaps because of ignorance, then employers will not be able to abrogate their responsibilities under employment law.

Teachers need to be cautious about contracts and use the experience and expertise of full-time union officers in examining contracts thoroughly. Contracts should not be taken on trust; there are far too many examples of abuses of contract law. It is far too easy to mislead employees in this area of the law.

Salaries

From September 2002, the previous distinction between good honours graduates and other graduates will be removed. This means that all new entrants to the profession who hold a degree or degree equivalent will commence on the new point one of the six-point salary spine (£17,628 as at September 2002). For experience inside or outside teaching, up to a maximum of five points may be allocated. Each September, a serving teacher who has worked at least 26 weeks in the previous 12 months will receive an additional spine point, subject to the maximum of spine point 6 being reached. These annual additional spine points are mandatory, provided that the teacher's performance is satisfactory. The onus is upon the school or the LEA to prove that a teacher's performance has been unsatisfactory. This means following a proper procedure and not simply deeming that an additional point is being withheld.

Experience gained outside teaching may include work experience or unremunerated activity such as bringing up a family. The allocation of such spine points is not mandatory; however, governing bodies should always take such experience into account when determining the starting salary of mature entrants.

The salary structure for teachers and head teachers was amended in September 2000, with further amendments being introduced in September 2002. The Main Pay Scale from September 2002 will consist of six points, £17,628 to £25,746. The Upper Pay Scale will consist of five points, £27,894 to £32,250. Although the unions would like progression up the Upper Pay Scale to be automatic, this is unlikely to be the case, since the DfES has suggested to head teachers that a teacher's performance must be sustained and substantial; however, no guidance has been given as to how to assess these criteria.

There are now (as at April 2002) five management allowances, ranging from £1,593 to £10,275, which are paid in addition to the teacher's salary on the Main Pay Scale or the Upper Pay Scale. These allowances should be paid for additional duties and responsibilities (which should be clearly defined in the job description). There are now five recruitment and retention allowances, ranging from £975 to £5,262. Largely in response to the very real problem of teacher shortages, there has been a significant increase in these allowances, of which there were previously only two or three. The Review Body reported that between January 2000 and January 2001, the number of vacancies had risen by 2,060 and the number of supply teachers had risen by over 5,000 between 1999 and 2001. These statistics from the Eleventh Report of the School Teachers Review Body indicate that there is a continuing problem with teacher shortages.

There are now two Special Education Allowances. The first provides an extra £1,626 and the second an extra £3,219. Teachers in special schools and special needs teachers in mainstream schools may receive one or both of these additional allowances.

Finally, on salaries, there are London Area Allowances, which are currently the subject of a dispute between the unions in the London area and the Secretary of State. The Inner London Allowance is £3,105, the Outer London Allowance, £2,043, the Fringe Allowance, £792 and the Inner London Area Supplement amounts to £822. When compared to allowances paid to the police who work in the capital, the amounts paid to teachers are approximately half.

Since September 2000, a new pay scale has been introduced for head teachers, deputy head teachers and assistant head teachers. This is called the Leadership Group with a range from £30,564 to £85,704. There are a suggested eight groups of schools with recommended ranges for the salaries that should be paid in those different groups.

It is recommended that before formally accepting a teaching post the spine point at which the teacher will be placed is established. All teachers are entitled to receive, on an annual basis, a statement of salary applicable to the post held. It is important therefore that salary is discussed at interview. If for some reason the salary point is not made clear at interview it is advisable to accept the post on a provisional basis, subject to salary and contract. This will then ensure a written offer of the post is made detailing salary point, with the breakdown of how that has been worked out, and the terms of the contract of employment.

All of the annual salaries quoted in this section contain an amount paid to all teachers to cover the cost of fees payable to the GTCs. In 2002, this amounted to £33.

Conclusion

Market forces applied to the education service have had a serious effect on the conditions of service of schoolteachers and on their salaries. It inevitably means local variations within the national framework; sometimes this local interpretation at school level can work to the advantage of teachers, sometimes not. One recent test of this is the manner in which the terms of DfEE Circular 2/98 *Reducing the Bureaucratic Burden on Teachers* (DfEE 1998) have been implemented in schools. The Secretary of State for Education and Employment, at the time, said, 'cutting unnecessary burdens on teachers helps us to raise standards in schools, and that is our top priority' (DfEE 1998, front cover). So conditions of service should have changed, hopefully this time to the benefit of teachers. However, the evidence would suggest that the workload of teachers is still excessive.

This is currently (at the time of writing) being addressed by a separate review exercise being conducted by the Review Body, which will report in April 2002. The Eleventh Report of the Review Body referred to the joint submission of the teacher unions on the issue of improvements in teachers' conditions of service. There was in this submission extensive reference to the Scottish Teachers' Agreement. Paragraph 38 of the Report of the Review Body states: 'The evidence also referred to the existence in the [Scottish] Agreement of minimum standards and entitlements with regard to working time and class contact time, as well as other improvments in conditions of service' (DfES, 2002b).

What is specifically required is a limitation on the current paragraph 59.8 within the STPACD 2001. This paragraph effectively means that a teacher's working time is open-ended in terms of performing the professional duties of the job. In practice, this means that teachers work regularly on average in excess of 55 hours per week during term time. If the Scottish model were to be applied in England and Wales, this would go a long way to reducing the workload on teachers, and perhaps make the profession more attractive to prospective teachers.

The profession needs the confidence to take control of its own destiny. The role of the newly established General Teaching Council (GTC) will need to be seen in the context of an education system, however, which a number of commentators (e.g. Cole 1998, 2002; Hatcher 1998; Allen *et al.* 1999; Hill 2001; Rikowski 2001) have suggested is witnessing burgeoning privatisation. In order to protect and advance the conditions of service of schoolteachers, a major role of GTCs and, of course, the teacher unions, should be to resist this trend.

Note

1. At the present time, 'permanent' only becomes significant after an employee has worked for an employer for a continuous period of one year. For this reason, some full-time union officials use the term 'ongoing' rather than 'permanent'.

References

Advisory, Conciliation and Arbitration Service (ACAS) (1998) *Code of Practice for Time Off for Trade Union Duties and Activities.* London: HMSO.

Allen, M., Cole, M. and Hatcher, R. (1999) *Business, Business, Business: the New Labour Agenda in Education.* London: Tufnell Press.

Cole, M. (1998) 'Globalization, Modernization and Competitiveness: a Critique of the New Labour Project in Education', *International Studies in Sociology of Education,* **8**(3).

Cole, M. (2002) 'New Labour, Globalization and Social Justice: the Role of Education', in P. McLaren, H. Sunker, G. Fischman (eds) *Critical Theories, Radical Pedagogies, and Global Conflicts.* Lanham, Maryland: Rowman and Littlefield.

Council of Local Education Authorities/Schoolteacher Committee (CLEA/ST) (1985) *Conditions of Service for Schoolteachers in England and Wales,* 2nd edn (the 'Burgundy Book'). Revised edn 2000.

DES (1990) Circular Number 7/90. *Management of the School Day.* London: HMSO.

DfEE (1998) Circular Number 2/98. *Reducing the Bureaucratic Burden on Teachers.* London: HMSO.

DfES (2002a) *Schoolteachers' Pay and Conditions Document.* (The 'Blue Book'.) London: HMSO.

DfES (2002b) Eleventh Report of Teachers' Review Body. London: HMSO.

Hatcher, R. (1998) 'Labour, Official School Improvement and Equality', *Journal of Educational Policy,* **13**(4), 485–99.

Hill, D. (2001) 'Global Capital, Neo-liberalism, and Privatization: the Growth of Educational Inequality', in D. Hill and M. Cole (eds) *Schooling and Equality: Fact, Concept and Policy.* London: Kogan Page.

Local Government Review [605] (1969). *Barnes v Hampshire County Council.*

National Union of Teachers (NUT) (1987) *Salaries and Superannuation Report 1987,* 153–63. London: NUT.

National Union of Teachers (NUT) (1995) *Research into the Issuing of Fixed-Term and Temporary Contracts on a Full- or Part-Time Basis with Particular Reference to Women.* London: NUT.

Rikowski, G. (2001) 'Schools: Building for Business', *Post-16 Educator,* **3**, 14–15.

Wragg, E. C. *et al.* (1998) *Teacher Competence Project: Occasional Paper No. 2.* Exeter: University of Exeter.

Appendix 1: Standards for advanced skills teachers

Excellent results or outcomes

1. As a result of the advanced skills teachers' teaching, pupils show consistent improvement in relation to prior and expected attainment; are highly motivated, enthusiastic and respond positively to challenge and high expectations; exhibit consistently high standards of discipline and behaviour; show a consistent track record of parental involvement and satisfaction.

Excellent subject or specialist knowledge

2. Advanced skills teachers must keep up to date in their subject or specialism; have a full understanding of connections and progression in the subject and use this in their teaching to ensure pupils make good progress; quickly understand pupils' perceptions and misconceptions from their questions and responses; understand information and communications technology in the teaching of their subject or specialism.

Excellent ability to plan

3. Advanced skills teachers must prepare lessons and sequences of lessons with clear objectives to ensure successful learning by all pupils; set consistently high expectations for pupils in their class and homework; plan their teaching to ensure it builds on the current and previous achievement of pupils.

Excellent ability to teach, manage pupils and maintain discipline

4. Advanced skills teachers must understand and use the most effective teaching methods to achieve the teaching objectives in hand; must display flair and creativity in engaging, enthusing and challenging groups of pupils; use questioning and explanation skilfully to secure maximum progress; must develop pupils' literacy, numeracy and information and communications technology skills as appropriate within their phase and context; are able to provide positive and targeted support for pupils who have special educational needs, are very able, are from ethnic minorities, lack confidence, have behavioural difficulties or are disaffected; must maintain respect and discipline; are consistent and fair.

Excellent ability to assess and evaluate

5. Advanced skills teachers must use assessment as part of their teaching to diagnose pupils' needs, set realistic and challenging targets for improvement and plan future teaching; improve their teaching through evaluating their own practice in relation to pupils' progress, school targets and inspection evidence.

Excellent ability to advise and support other teachers

6. Advanced skills teachers must provide clear feedback, good support and sound advice to others; are able to provide examples, coaching and training to help others

become more effective in their teaching; can help others to evaluate the impact of their teaching on raising pupils' achievements; are able to analyse teaching and understand how improvements can be made; have highly developed inter-personal skills which allow them to be effective in schools and situations other than their own; provide a role model for pupils and other staff through their personal and professional conduct; know how to plan and prioritise their own time and activity effectively; are highly respected and able to motivate others.

Source: DfES 2002a.

Appendix 2: Performance threshold standards

Knowledge and Understanding

1. Teachers should demonstrate that they have a thorough and up-to-date knowledge of the teaching of their subject and take account of wider curriculum developments which are relevant to their work.

Teaching and Assessment

2. Teachers should demonstrate that they consistently and effectively plan lessons and sequences of lessons to meet pupils' individual learning needs.
3. Teachers should demonstrate that they consistently and effectively use a range of appropriate strategies for teaching and classroom management.
4. Teachers should demonstrate that they consistently and effectively use information about prior attainment to set well-grounded expectations for pupils and monitor progress to give clear and constructive feedback.

Pupil progress

5. Teachers should demonstrate that, as a result of their teaching, their pupils achieve well relative to the pupils' prior attainment, making progress as good or better than similar pupils nationally. This should be shown in marks or grades in any relevant national tests or examinations, or school-based assessment for pupils where national tests and examinations are not taken.

Wider Professional Effectiveness

6. Teachers should demonstrate that they take responsibility for their professional development and use the outcomes to improve their teaching and pupils' learning.
7. Teachers should demonstrate that they make an active contribution to the policies and aspirations of the school.

Professional Characteristics

8. Teachers should demonstrate that they are effective professionals who challenge and support all pupils to do their best through:
(a) inspiring trust and confidence,
(b) building team commitment,

(c) engaging and motivating pupils,

(d) analytical thinking,

(e) positive action to improve the quality of pupils' learning.

Source: Annexe 1 from DfES 2002a.

Appendix 3: PART XII of the STPCAD – Conditions of employment of teachers other than head teachers

Exercise of general professional duties

56.1   Subject to paragraph 37.6, 38.2, 38.3 and 56.2, a teacher who is not a head teacher shall carry out the professional duties of a teacher as circumstances may require:

56.1.1   if he is employed as a teacher in a school, under the reasonable direction of the head teacher of that school;

56.1.2   if he is employed by an authority on terms under which he is not assigned to any one school, under the reasonable direction of that authority and of the head teacher of any school in which he may for the time being be required to work as a teacher.

56.2   A teacher who has failed satisfactorily to complete an induction period and who is employed pursuant to regulation 16(5) of the Induction Regulations must only carry out such limited teaching duties as the Secretary of State determines pursuant to that regulation.

Exercise of particular duties

57.1   Subject to paragraph 37.6, 38.2, 38.3, and 56.2 a teacher employed as a teacher (other than a head teacher) in a school shall perform, in accordance with any directions which may reasonably be given to him by the head teacher from time to time, such particular duties as may reasonably be assigned to him.

57.2   A teacher employed by an authority on terms such as those described in paragraph 56.1.2 shall perform, in accordance with any direction which may reasonably be given to him from time to time by the authority or by the head teacher of any school in which he may for the time being be required to work as a teacher, such particular duties as may reasonably be assigned to him.

Professional duties

58.   Subject to paragraph 37.6, 38.2, 38.3, and 56.2 the following duties shall be deemed to be included in the professional duties which a teacher (other than a head teacher) may be required to perform:

58.1   **Teaching:**

In each case having regard to the curriculum for the school:

58.1.1   planning and preparing courses and lessons;

58.1.2   teaching, according to their educational needs, the pupils assigned to him, including the setting and marking of work to be carried out by the pupil in school and elsewhere;

58.1.3   assessing, recording and reporting on the development, progress and attainment of pupils;

58.2   **Other activities:**

58.2.1   promoting the general progress and well-being of individual pupils and of any class or group of pupils assigned to him;

58.2.2   providing guidance and advice to pupils on educational and social matters and on their further education and future careers, including information about sources of more expert advice on specific questions; making relevant records and reports;

58.2.3   making records of and reports on the personal and social needs of pupils;

58.2.4   communictaing and consulting with the parents of pupils;

58.2.5   communicating and co-operating with persons or bodies outside the school; and

58.2.6   participating in meetings arranged for any of the purposes described above;

58.3   **Assessments and reports:**

providing or contributing to oral and written assessments, reports and references relating to individual pupils and groups of pupils;

58.4   **Appraisal:**

participating in arrangements made in accordance with regulations made under section 49 of the Education (No. 2) Act 1986[69] for the appraisal of his performance and that of other teachers;

58.5   **Review, induction, further training and development:**

58.5.1   reviewing from time to time his methods of teaching and programmes of work;

58.5.2   participating in arrangements for his further training and professional development as a teacher;

58.5.3   in the case of a teacher serving an induction period pursuant to the Induction Regulations, participating in arrangements for his supervision and training;

58.6   **Educational methods:**

advising and co-operating with the head teacher and other teachers (or any one or more of them) on the preparation and development of courses of study, teaching materials, teaching programmes, methods of teaching and assessment and pastoral arrangements;

58.7   **Discipline, health and safety:**

maintaining good order and discipline among the pupils and safeguard-

[69] 1986 c.61; the regulations currently in force under this provision are S.I. 1991/1511 amended by S.I. 1999/2261.

ing their health and safety both when they are authorised to be on the school premises and when they are engaged in authorised school activities elsewhere;

58.8 **Staff meetings:**

participating in meetings at the school which relate to the curriculum for the school or the administration or organisation of the school, including pastoral arrangements;

58.9 **Cover:**

58.9.1 subject to paragraph 58.9.2, supervising and so far as practicable teaching any pupils whose teacher is not available to teach them:

58.9.2 subject to the exceptions in paragraph 58.9.3, no teacher shall be required to provide such cover:

(a) after the teacher who is absent or otherwise not available has been so for three or more consecutive working days; or

(b) where the fact that the teacher would be absent or otherwise not available for a period exceeding three consecutive working days was known to the maintaining authority or, in the case of a school which has a delegated budget, to the governing body, for two or more working days before the absence commenced;

58.9.3 the exceptions are:

(a) he is a teacher employed wholly or mainly for the purpose of providing such cover ('a supply teacher');

(b) the authority or the governing body (as the case may be) have exhausted all reasonable means of providing a supply teacher to provide cover without success; or

(c) he is a full-time teacher at the school but has been assigned by the head teacher in the time-table to teach or carry out other specified duties (except cover) for less than 75 per cent of those hours in the week during which pupils are taught at the school;

58.10 **Public examinations:**

participating in arrangements for preparing pupils for public examinations and in assessing pupils for the purposes of such examinations; recording and reporting such assessments; and participating in arrangements for pupils' presentation for and supervision during such examinations;

58.11 **Management:**

58.11.1 contributing to the selection for appointment and professional development of other teachers and non-teaching staff, including the induction and assessment of new teachers and teachers serving induction periods pursuant to the Induction Regulations;

58.11.2 assisting the head teacher or an assessor in carrying out threshold assessments of other teachers for whom he has management responsibility;

58.11.3 co-ordinating or managing the work of other teachers; and

58.11.4 taking such part as may be required of him in the review, development and management of activities relating to the curriculum, organisation and pastoral functions of the school;

58.12   **Administration:**

58.12.1   participating in administrative and organisational tasks related to such duties as are described above, including the management or supervision of persons providing support for the teachers in the school and the ordering and allocation of equipment and materials; and

58.12.2   attending assemblies, registering the attendance of pupils and supervising pupils, whether these duties are to be performed before, during or after school sessions.

Working time

59.1   The provisions of this paragraph shall not apply to deputy head teachers, assistant head teachers, advanced skills teachers or to teachers employed to teach part-time and are subject to paragraphs 37.6, 38.2 and 38.3 and 59.2.

59.2   For the school year beginning in 2001:
          (a)   any reference in this paragraph to 195 days shall be read as a reference to 194 days;
          (b)   any reference to 190 days shall be read as a reference to 189 days; and
          (c)   any reference to 1265 hours shall be read as a reference to 1258.5 hours.

59.3   A teacher employed full-time, other than in the circumstances described in paragraph 59.5, shall be available for work for 195 days in any school year, of which 190 days shall be days on which he may be required to teach pupils in addition to carrying out other duties; and those 195 days shall be specified by his employer or, if the employer so directs, by the head teacher.

59.4   Such a teacher shall be available to perform such duties at such times and such places as may be specified by the head teacher (or, where the teacher is not assigned to any one school, by his employer or the head teacher of any school in which he may for the time being be required to work as a teacher) for 1265 hours in any school year, those hours to be allocated reasonably throughout those days in the school year on which he is required to be available for work.

59.5   Paragraphs 59.2 and 59.3 do not apply to such a teacher employed wholly or mainly to teach or perform other duties in relation to pupils in a residential establishment.

59.6   Time spent in travelling to or from the place of work shall not count against the 1265 hours referred to in paragraph 59.4.

59.7   Such a teacher shall not be required under his contract as a teacher to undertake midday supervision, and shall be allowed a break of reasonable length either between school sessions or between the hours of 12 noon and 2.00pm.

59.8 Such a teacher shall, in addition to the requirements set out in paragraphs 59.2 and 59.3, work such additional hours as may be needed to enable him to discharge effectively his professional duties, including, in particular, the marking of pupils' work, the writing of reports on pupils and the preparation of lessons, teaching material and teaching programmes. The amount of time required for this purpose beyond the 1265 hours referred to in paragraph 59.4 and the times outside the 1265 specified hours at which duties shall be performed shall not be defined by the employer but shall depend upon the work needed to discharge the teacher's duties.

Source: DfES 2002a (Part XII)

CHAPTER 9

Schoolteachers' legal liabilities and responsibilities

Jeff Nixon

'In loco parentis'

It is of paramount importance for teachers to be aware of the array of legislation that affects their work with pupils both inside and outside schools. The aim of this chapter is to provide a framework within which it will be possible to act sensibly and professionally with due regard to the law and teachers' responsibilities both in general and specifically.

Let us first look at the way in which the concept of teachers' responsibility towards pupils has changed in recent times. We are probably all aware of the infamous phrase '*in loco parentis*', which for many years served as a convenient shorthand way of describing a multitude of circumstances where teachers found themselves responsible for the welfare and well-being of children. Teachers should act in place of the parent (now we would say 'parent/carer') and in doing so act wisely and prudently. The problem with this formulation is that the wise and prudent parent/carer who has a brood of 30 to 35 children does not in reality exist. That old Latin phrase is too set in the past to be meaningful. Today, a higher expectation of teachers is apparent; an expectation that they will do a better job than some notional parent/carer may do.

It is interesting to examine the words of Mr Justice Hilbery when he defined the responsibility of teachers towards a group of pupils. In posing the question, 'What has a reasonably careful parent to do?', his response appears entrenched in an age that has long disappeared.

> Supposing a boy of yours has some other little boys, who are friends of his, coming to tea on a Saturday afternoon and you see them all playing in the garden. Suppose your garden roller happened to be there. Would you consider you had been neglectful of your duty to the parents of those other boys because, for five minutes, you had gone into the house and two of them had managed to pull the roller over the third? Would you think that, in those circumstances you had failed to exercise reasonable supervision as a parent? These things have got to be treated

as matters of common sense, not to put on [a teacher] any higher standard of care than that of a reasonable careful parent. If the boys were kept in cotton wool, some of them would choke themselves with it. They would manage to have accidents: we always did, members of the jury – we did not always have actions at law afterwards. You have to consider whether or not you would expect a head teacher to exercise such a degree of care that boys could never get into mischief. Has any reasonable parent yet succeeded in exercising such care as to prevent a boy getting into mischief and – if he did – what sort of boys should we produce? (Barrell and Partington (1985): at pages 438–9)

This example is a quaint illustration that demonstrates how much has changed in recent times. Any teacher who nipped to the staffroom, for whatever reason, for five minutes and left a class, where there was the potential for danger, would not be given much sympathy. If, in hoping to seek justification this passage from Justice Hilbery was quoted, the teacher would not be taken seriously and would probably become the subject of a disciplinary action, even if nothing of any consequence actually happened in the unattended classroom.

To take another example, as parents/carers, we would expect that when pupils are taken out on a school journey they would, at the very least, be counted on to the coach before departure, and counted off and on the coach at any stopping points and upon arrival at the destination, that they would be counted on to the coach for the return to school, counted off and on at any stopping point, and counted off at the end of the journey. You might also expect that this mundane exercise would be carried out by more than one person. Parents/carers, and the public generally, would be horrified if no counting was done at all; but it does happen.

As parents/carers become more aware of their rights under the law and the prospect of more cases going to the courts for consideration increases, it is inevitable that the tests applied to assess cases will become more and more rigorous. It is important, therefore, to consider tests for negligence in very general terms. For an action for negligence to succeed, three factors must be present: first, the defendant must owe a duty of care; second, by either act or omission, the defendant must fail to provide the said duty of care; third, damage must have occurred to the party or parties bringing the action.

Teachers' duty of care

There are three elements to the concept of a teachers' duty of care: the common law aspect, the statutory consideration; and the contractual obligation (for a discussion of this last element, see Chapter 8, where the 'Blue Book', the Schoolteachers' Pay and Conditions Document, was outlined in some detail).

The 'common law duty' was highlighted in *Lyes v Middlesex County Council* in 1962 (Local Government Review 1963) where the 'standard of care' expected of a teacher was held to be that of a person exhibiting the responsible mental qualities of a prudent parent in the circumstances of the school, rather than the home. It has been acknowledged that a teacher's duty of care to individual pupils is influenced by the subject or the activity being taught, the age of the children, the available resources and the size of the class. This can be clarified further by adding the proviso that, even though others may disagree, if it can be shown that the teacher acted in accordance with the views of a reputable body of opinion within the profession, the duty of care will have been discharged. The definition of the 'common law' duty of care may become even more sharply focused as progress is made to reduce the size of classes and with the establishment of the General Teaching Councils for England and Wales (GTCs).

Since September 2000 there has been established a GTC for England and a separate one for Wales; Scotland has had one since 1965. The GTCs have key powers over entry to the profession and the manner in which the profession conducts itself which will clearly impact upon individual teachers in relation to any issues that would fall into the category of misconduct. The GTCs will not have the powers that relate to pay and conditions; these issues will continue to be dealt with by the Review Body procedures outlined in the previous chapter.

With respect to the 'statutory duty of care', the Children Act 1989, Section 3, sub-section 5 defined the duty of care as doing 'what is reasonable in all circumstances of the case for the purpose of safeguarding and promoting the child's welfare'. Teachers who are entrusted with the care of children during the school day have this statutory duty. The Children Act stresses the paramountcy of the wishes and needs of the child, reflecting the law's current more child-focused approach. Rather than the old-fashioned idea that a child was owned by its parents and this parental authority of property rights was delegated to teachers during the school day, the child's ascertainable needs and wishes should be taken into account by the teacher and considered in the light of the child's age and level of understanding. The teacher needs to assess the risk of harm that could arise to a child in particular circumstances, and to consider the safeguarding of the child and the promotion of the child's welfare and interest. This approach is clearly much more complex than the simplistic doctrine of the child as the property of the parents and demonstrates again how outmoded the term 'in loco parentis' has become.

It should also be noted that head teachers are required by the 'Blue Book' to carry out professional duties in accordance with the provisions of educational legislation, education orders and regulations, articles of government of the school, any applicable trust deed, any scheme of local management approved or imposed by the Secretary of State and any rules, regulations and policies laid down by the governing body under delegated powers or by the employing authority. In addition, a head teacher is also bound by the terms and conditions of any contract of employment, which means in totality that the head teacher is responsible for the internal organisation, management and control of the school.

If the concept of the 'duty of care' appears to be a complicated matter when it refers to activities within the school, it becomes ever more complex when a teacher is engaged in leading or assisting with activities off the school site, such as educational visits, school outings or field trips. The law on negligence is particularly significant here; the legal liability of a teacher or head teacher for any injury which is sustained by a pupil on a school journey or excursion would be dependent upon the three tests for negligence outlined earlier. If a child suffered an injury as a direct result of some negligence or failure to fulfil the duty of care, the employer of the teacher or head teacher would be legally liable. This is because employers have vicarious liability for the negligence of employees at work. Consequently where legal claims arise following an accident to a pupil, and there is a suggestion of negligence on the part of the teacher, the claim will most likely be made against the LEA as the employer of the teacher or the governing body in the case of Voluntary Aided, Foundation schools, sixth-form colleges or independent schools, if the teacher was, at the time of the accident to the pupil or student, working in the course of employment. It is, however, possible for teachers to be fined (see Chapter 8).

The standard of care required of a teacher is that which, from an objective point of view, can reasonably be expected from teachers generally applying skill and awareness of children's problems, needs and susceptibilities. Under health and safety legislation the law expects a teacher to do everything that a parent/carer with care or concern for the safety and welfare of his or her own child would do, bearing in mind that being responsible for up to 20 pupils or students at a time in an out-of-school activity is very different from looking after a family. The legal duty of care expected of an individual teacher can best be summed up by saying it is that which a caring teaching profession would expect of itself.

In practice this means that a teacher must ensure supervision of pupils throughout the journey or visit according to professional standards and common sense. Reasonable steps must be taken to avoid exposing pupils to dangers which are foreseeable and beyond those with which the particular pupils can reasonably be expected to cope. This does not imply constant 24-hour direct supervision while away on a residential field trip. The need for direct supervision has to be assessed by reference to the risks involved in the activity being undertaken. It is not enough merely to give instructions. The possibility that these instructions may be challenged by one or more of the pupils or students has to be taken into account, together with the risks the pupils may encounter if instructions are disobeyed. Equally pupils' *individual* levels of understanding and responsibilities have to be taken into account.

Where teachers believe that a journey or visit has not been adequately prepared or organised, they should not be expected to participate. It is important to note the terms in which the teacher's concern is expressed. If it is seen as a refusal to participate, in some circumstances this could be viewed as breach of contract or as an act of insubordination and could possibly lead to disciplinary procedures. The onus is on the teacher to demonstrate that there are proper professional and strategic reasons which give rise to the belief that there is a lack of preparation and organisation. Where the journey is one organised from within the school, responsibility for ensuring that proper preparation has been made and that proper supervision will be provided is ultimately that of the head teacher. Therefore it is the responsibility of head teachers to prohibit journeys and visits if they are not satisfied with the preparation and organisation of such journeys and visits.

Satisfying the duty of care absolves teachers from legal liability. However, sometimes accidents occur as a result of the fault of someone with no organising or supervising responsibility for the journey; for example, the bus company used for the trip. Should an accident occur where pupils and/or teachers sustain injury as a result of some defect in the vehicle, the bus company would of course be liable.

Some accidents are pure accidents, not reasonably foreseen and not the result of negligence on anyone's part; if no one is responsible then there can be no liabilities. Consequently liability goes with fault. In the case of a pure accident no one bears liability. Schools and LEAs will be covered in this eventuality by 'no-fault insurance'. Some LEAs act as loss adjusters for their own insurance procedures and settlement of a particular claim does not carry with it a notion of liability on the part of the LEA as employer. Recently an Appeal Court judge, deliberating on a case for damages following an accident, said something quite profound given the type of 'blame culture' we now encounter relentlessly in society. She said, 'Sometimes, somethings happen that are, quite simply, nobody's fault.' We would all do well to heed these words of wisdom before rushing to the law to attempt to apportion blame.

The Health and Safety at Work Act 1974

The Health and Safety at Work Act 1974 is one of the major pieces of legislation of the 1970s. It was and still is 'enabling legislation' and, since the onset of more and more Directives from Europe, the whole health and safety arena has become more and more crowded with regulation, codes of practice and written recording of such matters as substances that are hazardous to health, dangerous occurrences and risk assessments. It would be impossible for teachers to be familiar with everything connected with the Act; it is far too extensive a field. However, certain elements of the legislation are very important for teachers, particularly Sections 7 and 8 of the Act. The main responsibility under the 1974 Act rests with the employer, who has to take reasonable care for the health and safety of employees and others who are on their premises. This includes not only the children, teachers and support staff, but also parents/carers and other visitors to the school; in particular those making deliveries.

However, all employees have a duty under the Act to take reasonable care for the health and safety of themselves and others who may be affected by their acts or omissions at work. Consequently teachers have a duty to take reasonable care of both their own and their pupils' health and safety at school. The law also requires employees to act in a cooperative manner with respect to any guidance provided by the employer to assist in maintaining a safe working environment. For teachers, this means following carefully school-based or LEA guidance on policy and procedure, and ensuring they are familiar with such practices. It means in practice that teachers should act with reasonable care at all times and apply good sense to everything they do, including not taking any unnecessary risks or doing anything that is potentially dangerous to themselves, the children and parents/carers who may be helping out either in school or on out-of-school activities. There is a duty on all employees to report any hazards and potentially dangerous incidents at work; teachers should make themselves familiar with the reporting and recording system in their school (e.g. the accident report book). There may also be a need to report certain types of accident to the Health and Safety Executive for possible investigation, consideration of prosecution and recommendations to be implemented to avoid a similar occurrence. Occupational injuries should also be reported to the local office of the Department of Social Security; delay in reporting such injuries could result in benefits being lost in the short and long term. To facilitate all this, each school should have a trained and well-informed Health and Safety representative. The unions do encourage members to take on such a role, and provide comprehensive training in the rights and responsibilities associated with such a role. However, the unions discourage members becoming Health and Safety *officers* as, under the Act, such individuals are much more liable legally for their acts and omissions; representatives are not liable for the things they do or do not do as representatives.

Health and Safety representatives' responsibilities are towards the trade union members they represent only and their job is to ensure that information is made available, accidents and the aftermath are properly recorded and acted upon, investigations are carried out, where appropriate, and inspections of the premises are undertaken on a regular basis (at least once a term in school time). It is important for health and safety representatives to encourage everyone to report even what might seem to be a minor matter that may simply require cleaning up, or a small inexpensive repair. Seemingly minor matters can cause serious accidents. The most frequently recorded accidents in schools involve slipping, tripping and falling – usually because of a patch of wet or because rubbish on the floor has not been cleared away. Teachers themselves can contribute to their own accidents; the most common problem tends to be piling up furniture, attempting to mount displays or to change broken light bulbs on wobbly chairs or wobbly tables. The first questions anyone investigating such accidents will ask are why did the teacher not use proper equipment and, with respect to the light bulb, why, when it is not their responsibility, was a teacher changing a light bulb in the first place?

Teachers who undertake particular specialist activities, such as the instruction or teaching of swimming, trampolining, canoeing and rock climbing, are required to hold particular qualifications. There may also be a requirement within the qualification to regularly update the skills required in order to continue teaching and supervising the activity. Should there be any doubt about the need for an extra qualification or the need for updating, teachers should not take on the activity until the appropriate professional body or association concerned has been consulted. The health, safety and welfare of children in the care of teachers is a fundamental requirement. Parents/carers entrust their children to the schools and to teachers in particular; they do not expect children to come to any harm there.

Discipline and detention

Since April 1998, LEAs have to have 'behaviour support plans', which incorporate a statement setting out arrangements for dealing with pupils with behavioural difficulties, including the help they are able to offer schools in dealing with such difficulties, and in generally promoting good discipline. These plans must be published. Since September 1998, governing bodies of LEA schools must set out a framework for schools' discipline policies. This is to comply with Section 5 of the Education Act 1997. This means in practice that head teachers must draw up the school's discipline policy and make it known to pupils, parents/carers and staff at least once a year. DfES Circular 10/99 provides guidance on behaviour, discipline and detention.

Schools will now have a legal right to detain a pupil after the end of a school session, without parental consent, as long as the school provides the parent/carer with at least 24 hours' written notice. For this to be lawful, the head teacher must have made it known generally within the school and to have brought to the attention of parents/carers that detention as a sanction might be imposed. The detention must be imposed by the head teacher or other authorised teacher, and must be regarded as reasonable; in other words, it must be seen as a proportionate punishment. Any special circumstances relevant to the particular pupil must be taken into account. This would include the pupil's age, special needs, religious requirements and travel arrangements. The time of year may also be a consideration in some cases. The 24 hours' notice can be given to parents/carers by post, via the pupils or by fax.

Finally, with respect to fixed period exclusions, head teachers have the right to exclude pupils for fixed periods of up to 45 days per year; previously the fixed period was 15 days per term. In addition, the appeals procedure on pupil exclusion gives the school the right to be represented at appeal hearings. The committee considering the appeal must take account of the interests of other pupils and staff at the school before determining that a pupil should be reinstated. If the school's discipline policy contains specific examples of the sort of behaviour that may lead to exclusion, whether this is to be a temporary or permanent exclusion, these will be important evidence for an appeal hearing to consider. This change in the law should see an end to those unfortunate situations where a school has permanently excluded a pupil, normally for violent behaviour, only to find that an appeal committee has determined that the pupil has the right to return. When this happens it often leads to the members of teaching unions in the school being balloted on their willingness to refuse to teach such a pupil. In a small number of cases this has led to some adverse publicity with a pupil's name being made known to the media, with some individuals using the situation for their own personal ends or for the organisation they represent. Making a particular child a cause célèbre is not the right approach, and the new provision will at least create a more balanced approach to the decision-making process. Confidentiality should be an important component.

Confidentiality

Section 1.8 of the TTA requirements (TTA 2002) covers 'the statutory framework relating to teachers' responsibilities'. This would include an awareness of paragraphs 26 and 27 of Circular 10/95 which specifically mention the issue of confidentiality in relation to child protection procedures. It is important for student teachers to develop an ability to judge when to take advice on this and all teachers need to be aware that it is frequently not possible to give an undertaking that everything said in a conversation between a teacher and a pupil can remain confidential. It is important for all teachers to be aware that it is frequently not possible to give a pupil an undertaking that everything that is said in a conversation between a teacher and a pupil can remain confidential. Should the teacher be given information by a pupil that would be covered by child protection procedures, then the teacher would have to pass on that information either to the head teacher or the designated child protection officer. If the teacher remained unsure about any aspect of such a conversation with a pupil, then, clearly, advice should be sought from an appropriate colleague: the teacher should inform the pupil that the matter is being referred to the head teacher or other senior member of staff within the school who deals with child protection procedures. Teachers may also need to seek advice when requests are made for formal assessments or when providing information under the SEN (Special Educational Needs) Code of Practice (DfES 2001).

Appropriate physical contact and restraint

DfEE Circular 10/95, *Protecting Children from Abuse* (DfEE 1995), provides guidance about physical contact with pupils or students. Appropriate points of that guidance have now been incorporated into Section 550A of the Education Act 1996 (subject of a later section of this chapter). The relevant paragraphs of the circular are quoted here. These were drawn up after consultation with the teacher organisations.

> It is unnecessary and unrealistic to suggest that teachers should touch pupils only in emergencies. Particularly with younger pupils, touching them is inevitable and can give welcome reassurance to the child. However, teachers must bear in mind that even perfectly innocent actions can sometimes be misconstrued. Children may find being touched uncomfortable or distressing for a variety of reasons. It is important for teachers to be sensitive to a child's reaction to physical contact and to act appropriately. It is also important not to touch pupils, however casually, in ways or on parts of the body that might be considered indecent.

> Employers and senior staff have a responsibility to ensure that professional behaviour applies to relationships between staff and pupils or students, that all staff are

clear about what constitutes appropriate behaviour and professional boundaries, and that those boundaries are maintained with the sensitive support and supervision required. That is important in all schools, but residential institutions need to be particularly mindful of this responsibility as do individuals in circumstances where there is one to one contact with pupils, for example, in the teaching of music or extra curricular activities.

Teachers are considered to occupy a position of trust in relation to pupils and this may appear to be an obvious point to make; however, under the terms of the Sexual Offences (Amendment) Act 2000, a criminal offence is committed when a teacher embarks upon a relationship of a sexual nature with a pupil who is under the age of 18.

The offence can result in a custodial sentence upon conviction; any teacher who was convicted of such an offence would undoubtedly be placed on List 99, which is maintained by the DfES, and which contains the names of all those people who have been prohibited from working with children and young people.

Schools may find it helpful to agree in consultation with the LEA or Area Child Protection Committee (ACPC) a code of conduct for staff to reduce the risk of allegations being made. Some LEAs have already drawn up such codes which are recommended to schools. Where a school agrees such a code, it should be made known to parents/carers to help avoid any misunderstandings.

There have been recently a number of well-publicised cases that relate to teachers, child protection and misconduct cases. Some of these have concentrated on teachers being the subject of false or malicious allegations made by parents/carers and/or children. The length of time teachers are suspended from duty while child protection procedures are applied has also given cause for concern, so much so that a number of Regional Co-ordinators were appointed during 2001 to ensure procedures are not subject to any unnecessary delay to avoid teachers who are under investigation being left in a state of 'limbo'. Clearly, LEAs and governing bodies have responsibilities to protect children from harm and they need to be vigilant in their approach to these responsibilities. However, there is also a duty of care towards the individual teacher who is the subject of any enquiry and LEAs, Heads and Governing Bodies must not forget this. Often the needs of the teacher, who is away from the school community because of the suspension while the investigation is conducted, are considered not to be a priority, furthermore the teacher's absence from the school community leads to rumour, gossip and often unfounded speculation. This frequently makes it very difficult indeed to reintegrate the teacher even when the investigation either exonerates the individual or permits a return to the school community after the disciplinary procedures have concluded.

The GTCs also have roles to play in relation to the teacher misconduct and competence issues. The establishment of the GTCs means that the teaching profession is much more self-regulatory although for certain serious criminal convictions, and being placed on the Sex Offenders' Register would be one such example, a person's right to teach can be taken away directly by the DfES.

Whereas before the introduction of the GTCs all misconduct cases were referred to the Teacher Misconduct Unit and decisions about whether a teacher could continue to practise were taken by that Unit, in consultation with the Secretary of State, now less serious cases of misconduct and appeals relating to the failure of the Induction period will be dealt with by the Professional Conduct Committee of the GTC. In much the same way as doctors and lawyers can be 'struck off' by their professional bodies, the GTCs will have the power to de-register a teacher, subject, of course, to the usual rights of the teacher concerned making representations to the GTC.

Since 1998, provisions contained in Section 4 of the Education Act 1996 have clarified the position in relation to the use of physical force by teachers. Under the headline, 'Teachers Now Allowed to Hold, Push and Pull Unruly Pupils', the *Observer*'s education correspondent, Martin Bright, reported in the 26 July 1998 edition that the clarification was thought necessary because many teachers believed they were not allowed any contact of a physical nature. The General Secretary of the NUT, Doug McAvoy, was quoted as saying, 'This is sensible, straightforward advice that will help relieve the threats of legal action that hang over teaching staff.'

The relevant section of the Act, S550A, defines the powers of members of staff to restrain pupils or students. Staff can use such force as is reasonable in the circumstances to prevent the pupil from doing or continuing to:

(a) commit any offence;
(b) cause personal injury to or damage to the property of any person (including him or herself); or
(c) engage in any behaviour prejudicial to the maintenance of good order and discipline at the school or among any of its pupils, whether that behaviour occurs in a teaching session or elsewhere.

These circumstances apply where a member of staff of a school is:

(a) on the premises of the school; or
(b) elsewhere at a time when, as a member of staff, he or she has lawful control or charge of the pupil concerned. (DfEE (1998b) Circular 10/98, para. 10, p. 4)

The use of corporal punishment is excepted from these provisions as it was abolished in the maintained sector in August 1986.

The term 'member of staff' is defined as any teacher who works at the school, and any other person who, with the authority of the head teacher, has lawful control or charge of pupils at the school. 'Offence' is qualified by the caveat that under a certain age a child may not be capable of committing an offence.[1] The interpretation of this section of the law, therefore, is open to conjecture; the initial assessment and judgement of the teacher and the subsequent course of action adopted will be critical in assessing whether the amount of force used is reasonable. This will also be dependent upon a number of variables such as the age and size of the pupil and how much the teacher knows about the pupil. Other variables may be relevant; for example, whether the pupil concerned suffers from any pre-existing medical condition that may or may not have been known to the member of staff concerned. Restraining, by use of physical force, a pupil/student who suffers from brittle bone disease, for example, may not be considered a reasonable option in the circumstances.

Before the implementation of the Act, force was allowed in an emergency only; where pupils placed themselves at risk of physical injury, where pupil actions placed others at risk of physical injury and where damage to property could be limited by the use of restraint, without endangering the physical safety of pupils, staff or members of the public. The new provisions make clear that teachers and other authorised members of staff are entitled to intervene in other, less extreme, situations.

There is no definition in the Act of what constitutes 'reasonable force'. The interpretation of this is crucial for teachers and others defending their actions. It must be emphasised that the use of any degree of force is unlawful if the particular circumstances do not warrant it. The degree of force should be in proportion to the circumstances and seriousness of the behaviour or consequences it is intended to prevent. The level and duration of the force used should be the minimum necessary to achieve the desired result, such as to restore safety.

In some circumstances it will, of course, be inadvisable for a teacher to intervene without help, particularly where a number of pupils are involved and where pupils are older and more physically mature. Unless this was considered, the teacher might be at risk of injury and clearly this should be avoided.

Although the new provisions do not specifically mention the failure to take appropriate action, in circumstances which merit the use of reasonable force, such failure could be regarded as seriously as overreacting. This means that it is no longer possible to argue that it is a safer option for a member of staff to do nothing or to take very limited action, when to take some action would restore safety. As far as a teacher's duty of care is concerned, an omission can be significant if there were to be a subsequent claim for negligence. Having said that, a teacher would not be expected to intervene to restore safety, at all costs, to the personal safety of the teacher concerned. It is a matter for professional judgement that may need to stand up to detailed analysis and justification at a later time.

In 1994, the DfEE provided specific guidance on the physical restraint and education of children with emotional and behavioural difficulties (EBD) contained in Circular 9/94. Schools are required to have clear written policies on controls, restrictions and sanctions that can be used in dealing with EBD pupils/students and a positive approach is encouraged where intervention by teachers is based upon reward rather than punishment.

There is an acknowledgement in the circular, however, that difficulties in relation to EDB pupils are likely to be more severe and occur more frequently than with other children. Circular 9/94 advises:

Physical contact and restraint should never be used in anger, and teachers should seek to avoid any injury to the child. They are not expected to restrain a child if by doing so they will put themselves at risk. Brief periods of withdrawal away from the point of conflict into a calmer environment may be more effective for an agitated child than holding or physical restraint. Parents with children in special schools should be told how restraint is being exercised. Children who require complex or repeated physical management should have a prescribed, written handling policy. Staff dealing with them should be trained in proper and safe methods of restraint. (pp. 37, 38)

The Department of Health has issued guidance entitled 'Permissible Forms of Control in Children's Residential Care' (April 1993). This guidance is designed to cover young people living in Children's Homes, rather than in schools, but offers positive and practical advice to staff on the care and control of young people in residential accommodation. (p. 38)

Section 550A of the Education Act 1996 applies equally to EDB children.

The National Union of Teachers recommends that all incidents of restraint should be logged in a record book provided for that purpose and regularly monitored by a senior member of staff. The record should be contemporaneous and sufficiently detailed to help in any later investigation or complaint. It is advisable to inform parents/carers of any recorded incident. Since September 1998, all schools are required to have a behaviour policy which may well include guidance on the use of physical restraint involving touching, pushing, pulling and holding. Teachers will need to be made familiar with the school's policy and ensure they act within its terms at all times.

Training in methods of restraint may be considered appropriate for some staff and for certain types of school; however, the training provided should be appropriate and suitable people should be involved in its provision. A few years ago a residential special school that had encountered a number of students, mainly adolescent boys, exhibiting aggressive and challenging behaviour, brought in some prison officers on a training day to give instruction in physical restraint. The whole staff, teaching and support staff received the training. Afterwards the incidence of restraint increased dramatically and the injuries to students also gave cause for concern. Physical restraint and punishment almost became synonymous in the school and it is not surprising that shortly after an LEA inquiry into the school and its climate of indiscipline, it was recommended for closure.

Sex, 'race' and disability discrimination

Under the Sex Discrimination Act 1975 and the Race Relations Act 1976, it is unlawful to discriminate against a person on grounds of sex or marital status, or on racial grounds. The latter includes 'race', colour, nationality, citizenship, ethnic or national origins. It is unlawful to discriminate against a person directly or indirectly.

Direct discrimination

Direct discrimination is where, in similar circumstances, a person is treated less favourably, because of his or her 'race' or sex than the way in which another person of the opposite sex or different 'race' would be treated. Direct discrimination takes many forms. In the treatment of pupils and students, for example, it may vary from crude remarks to subtle differences in assessment, expectation, provision and treatment. It may be unconscious or even well meaning; however, it is still unlawful. Racial or sexual harassment is also a form of direct discrimination. Rights exist on 'race' and sex discrimination when candidates apply for posts and during the interview and other selection processes. This means that shortlisting and questions at interview must not contravene the legislation. The woman candidate who was asked at interview for the Head of Technology Department how she would deal with all the reactionary men who currently worked in the department suffered an incidence of sex discrimination on two counts: first, the terms of the question itself and second, the woman claimed that the question was discriminatory and sexist because the same question could not be put to a man and because it challenged her as a woman, rather than as a professional. She was the only candidate who was asked the question, as all the other candidates were men (NUT 1991a: 25).

Indirect discrimination

Indirect discrimination is more complex. It occurs when a requirement or condition, although applied equally, is such that a considerably smaller proportion of a particular racial group or sex can comply with it and when this cannot be objectively justified. The phrase 'objectively justifiable' means in an educational context that the condition or requirement cannot be justifiable on educational or other grounds. It has to be a question of examining the facts and the reason for the objective justification put forward in each and every case. An example of this is a case that reached the House of Lords (*Mandla and Mandla v Lee and Park Grove Private School Limited.* 1983 Industrial Relations Law Reports 109 HL) and involved the requirement to wear a cap as part of a school uniform. Although applied equally to all pupils and students, it had the effect of excluding Sikh boys from a particular school and this was not justifiable on educational grounds and, therefore, constituted unlawful indirect racial discrimination.

In schools, discrimination is specifically unlawful with respect to the terms of admission. Schools must not refuse to admit pupils or to employ staff on grounds of 'race' or sex. In addition, any arrangement that does not afford pupils equal access to benefits, facilities or services is also unlawful. Finally, it is against the law to exclude pupils from school or to subject them to any other detriment on grounds of sex or 'race'. The law makes an exception for single-sex schools although in doing so, it stipulates that the facilities available should be no less favourable than those in any other school in a given LEA.

The Commission for Racial Equality and the Equal Opportunities Commission have both issued Codes of Practice on the elimination of discrimination and organisations such as the National Union of Teachers publish, from time to time, pamphlets and research findings on a variety of equal opportunities issues (see, for example, NUT 1988, 1989a,b,c; 1991a,b, 1992, 1995, 2002). Any complaints against schools or LEAs concerning discrimination can be made to the Secretary of State for Education and Skills or, if a legal redress is sought, one can go to the county court. Complaints by employees or potential employees can be brought, without any need for a qualifying period, to Employment Tribunals in cases that relate to sex and race discrimination.

Race Relations (Amendment) Act 2000

Following the Stephen Lawrence Inquiry, the Race Relations Act 1976 was amended to assist public authorities in promoting race equality in all aspects of their work. The Commission for Race Equality (CRE) sent to all schools a draft guide and Race Equality Standards (*Learning for All*) providing advice on how schools are able to meet their statutory duties.

The General Duty section of the Act has three parts:

- eliminate unlawful racial discrimination
- promote equality of opportunity
- promote good relations between people from different racial backgrounds.

In relation to schools this means that policies and statements covering admissions, assessments, raising attainment levels, curriculum matters, discipline, guidance and support, and staff selection and recruitment, should all have elements which address the three parts of the General Duty. Schools have to bear in mind that the size of the ethnic minority population does not matter; racial equality is important even when there are no minority pupils or staff in a school or local community.

Schools must have a written statement of policy for promoting race equality by 31 May 2002 and, as soon as is practicable, arrangements for assessing the impact of policies on pupils, staff and parents, and a system of monitoring the operation of the policies paying particular attention to the levels of attainment of pupils from ethnic minority groups. The Race Equality Policy may be a clearly identifiable and easily available part of the school's policy on equal opportunities or the policy on inclusion; there should also be a clear link between the policy and the school's action plan or the School Improvement Plan.

Such policies and planning should become an integral part of the development of the school and its existing decision-making processes; the Governing body, therefore, plays a vital role in ensuring that the school meets it statutory duties in relation to promoting racial equality. Parents, pupils and staff need to know what the policy says and what it means for them. The questions which schools will need to ask on this amended legislation would include:

- Does the school help all its pupils to achieve as much as they can and do pupils gain the most from what is on offer?
- Which groups of pupils are underachieving and what are the reasons for this?
- Are the policies of the school having a positive impact on pupils, parents and staff from different racial groups?
- How are differences explained and justified? Are there explanations and justifications which have a basis in non-racial grounds like difficulties in the English language?
- Are the aims of each policy addressing the different needs of different groups? Do these aims lead to action on specific points like extra tuition or preventative measures to obviate racist incidents?
- Does the school prepare pupils for living in a multicultural society, promoting racial equality and harmony, and preventing or dealing with racism?

In attempting to address these questions the school will at least begin the process of complying with the General Duty contained within the Act. More importantly, the school and the community it serves will be laying down guiding principles which will hopefully lay the firm foundations for a more tolerant and fair society committed to equal opportunities for all.

The Disability Discrimination Act 1995

The Disability Discrimination Act (DDA), introduced in 1995, addresses discrimination in employment and in the provision of goods and services. It abolishes the employment quota of 3 per cent for disabled people established under the Disabled Persons (Employment) Act 1944. This quota system, whereby employers had to employ a minimum percentage of registered disabled people, was introduced towards the end of the Second World War when many service men and women were returning to the labour market and some had suffered disabling injuries during wartime service. The 1995 Act covers temporary and part-time staff as well as permanent and full-time staff.

Section 5 sub-section 1 of the Act states that 'an employer discriminates against a disabled person if, for any reason relating to their disability, the employer treats them less favourably than he treats or would treat others not having the disability and he cannot show that the treatment is justified' (DDA 1995, cited in TUC 1996: 2).

Teachers need to be aware of this not only in relation to disabled pupils in their care and in the interests of fostering greater awareness on the part of all the children about the needs, perceptions and feelings of disabled people, but also in relation to the employment of disabled young people when they leave school and enter the world of work.

Moreover, schools need to be regarded as places of work for disabled people (both children and adults) and the 'reasonable adjustments' section of the legislation is particularly relevant in this regard. Employers have a duty to make such reasonable adjustments to the workplace, work equipment or organisation of work where disabled employees or applicants need them because of their disability. Victimisation is also unlawful under the Act and employers must not take action against any person (disabled or not) who uses the provisions of the Act or appears as a witness at a tribunal hearing or gives evidence during an internal hearing.

A disability is defined as 'a physical or mental impairment which has a substantial and long term adverse effect on the ability to carry out normal day-to-day activities' (DDA 1995, cited in TUC 1996: 3). An impairment is one that has existed for 12 months or more, can reasonably be expected to last 12 months or more, or can reasonably be expected to last for the rest of a person's life. The impairment can be related to mobility, manual dexterity, physical coordination, continence, and the ability to lift, carry or move everyday objects. It can also be connected to speech, hearing or eyesight, memory, ability to concentrate, learn or understand. Some impairments will need medication or specific equipment. People with a learning or mental disability are covered by the DDA particularly when there is a substantial or long-term effect on the ability to carry out normal day-to-day activities.

The Act does not apply to employers with fewer than 20 employees, so the only schools which are not covered by the provisions are very small Church schools or very small Foundation schools where the governing body is the employer and the total number of employees who work at the school is less than 20.

Employment discrimination under the terms of the Act takes place when an employer treats a disabled person less favourably than others for a reason which relates to the disability of the disabled person. If the reason for less favourable treatment was not related to the disability then that would prevent a claim being pursued. However, the reason does not have to be the disability itself; if it is *related* to the person's disability, it is discrimination. For example, refusing to appoint a teacher with a facial disfigurement, not because of the disfigurement, but because it is claimed children might be frightened or upset, would still count as discriminatory.

Probably the most controversial area in the definition of discrimination is the part which deals with justifiable discrimination. The TUC is extremely unhappy about this concept and believes such discrimination can never be justified. As case law develops on this point and others, it may become clearer what this part of the legislation actually means in practice. In the meantime, negotiation and agreements on good equal opportunities policies, procedures and practices will have to be sufficient safeguards against employers using this part of the legislation to abrogate their responsibilities.

The Act applies to disabled applicants for jobs as well as to disabled employees. So the recruitment practices of governing bodies must be in keeping with the legislation. The selection of the best candidate must be based on an objective assessment of the candidate's ability to do the job and in many, if not all, cases the disability of any candidate will be irrelevant unless, of course, the 'reasonable adjustments' section of the legislation is relevant. Indeed this may only become applicable when an employer takes on an employee who is disabled in some way or an existing employee reports an impairment that has lasted 12 months or is expected to last 12 months or longer. Examples that are given about reasonable adjustments include making alterations to premises, reallocation of work, transfer to another job or site, changing a disabled person's working hours, permitting reasonable absence from work for rehabilitation, assessment or treatment, providing training, modifying or acquiring equipment or providing special instruction manuals, providing a reader or interpreter and, finally, providing a disabled person with supervision and guidance in fulfilling the requirements of the job (all these examples cover all employment, not just teaching).

There are a number of tests that may help in making a judgement about whether an adjustment is reasonable or not. First, any action must be effective by significantly reducing the disadvantage the disabled person would otherwise face. Second, the financial and other costs must be reasonable, given the resources of the organisation concerned and any action must be practicable for the employer in the specific circumstances. Last, consideration should be given to financial or other help that is available to the employer from outside agencies such as the Employment Service or charities. The Placement, Assessment and Counselling Teams (PACTS), a specialist branch of the Employment Service, may well provide advice at the local Job Centre.

The DDA is enforced by the employer's grievance procedure, and the Employment Tribunal system. Cases are beginning to be reported where disabled employees have successfully won several thousands of pounds in compensation, when tribunals have accepted that discrimination has occurred in terms of the provisions of the DDA. Much of the legislation is subject to interpretation, so teachers will need to seek advice and support in pursuing claims under the Act and will undoubtedly look to the unions for assistance with this as they do with other issues that relate to employment, conditions of service, educational and professional matters.

The Human Rights Act 1998

All workers in the UK have been covered by the Human Rights Act 1998 with the incorporation into domestic legislation of the European Convention on Human Rights (ECHR). This Convention and the legislation will develop over time so that account can be taken of case-law precedents and the way societies across the European Community change and evolve; those who wrote the Convention were keen for it to become 'a living instrument' which would act as a benchmark for making judgements about human rights issues. This would cover a wider range of discrimination issues than we have been used to in UK legislation and that is why it has been added to the list of legislation that newly qualified teachers should be familiar with and hopefully understand.

Equality issues for the future

The Government is also consulting on a range of other equality issues which will inform future legislation outlawing discrimination at work on the grounds of age, religion and sexual orientation. The consultation exercise will raise a number of important questions, including many which have been part of educational debate down the years; for example, whether the state education system should be secular in character or whether the number of 'Faith' schools should be increased. Other more general questions relate to employment law: should workers be forced to retire at a particular age? Are schemes like the statutory redundancy payments formula, which are currently based on age and length of service, discriminatory if the law is changed to include a person's age as a factor in determining discrimination? Should there be a single Equality Act and one equality Commission covering all of the discrepancies that exist in dealing with people who are different in some way, whether this is because of sexual orientation, gender, ethnic minority, age, religion or disability? The concept of an equality Act covering all of these factors appears to be a long-term aim of the Government. However, many who have already suffered the effects of discrimination in whatever form will feel changes in the law are long overdue.

Conclusion

Becoming professional is one thing; remaining professional is another. The days when the acquiring of a certificate to teach for life (or up to 40 years) are gone. The rate of change is so rapid and dramatic that the student teachers educated in the early part of the twenty-first century may not be equipped to function effectively well into the new millennium unless, and this is the important part for Government to understand, time is made available and built into the system for serving teachers to be given the opportunity for extensive professional development, education and training. Examples of good practice are already up and running with courses like the 'Keeping In Touch with Teaching' schemes. These are normally run by LEAs and are open to any teacher who wishes to return to the profession after a break in service, usually following absence for family reasons. There are also many successful Returnees' courses that LEAs and training institutions organise.

There are also examples now of the unions offering members not only training in matters that relate to union work but, increasingly, courses that assist in the continuing professional development of members. The NUT is at the forefront of this development, and the TUC is keen to encourage union members to become Learning Representatives, and to work alongside and within the recently formed Learning and Skills Councils. For example, the South East Region of the TUC recently set up a Sussex Union Learning Forum to promote the concept of lifelong learning amongst union members.

Perhaps, in the education service, in order to prepare adequately for the future, we might look back to the recommendations of the James Report, written almost 30 years ago. This important analysis of teacher education and the needs of the profession suggested a regular system of sabbatical terms or years dependent upon length of service. For example, a teacher with seven years' experience could look forward to a year's sabbatical which could provide valuable time for retraining and battery recharging. Money spent on that rather than on the introduction of the 'advanced skills teacher' would target resources in a more constructive and supportive way for the teaching profession and bring to the education service a precise strategy to improve the overall performance of practitioners, ensure there was adequate time for professional thinking and development and provide a substantial boost to morale, as well as making the teaching profession more attractive to potential recruits. While it may be true that 'everyone remembers a good teacher', a system must be devised whereby good teachers are not burnt out in a short time-scale. The implementation of this recommendation of the James Report is long overdue.

Note

1. The James Bulger murder case, in which two 10-year-old boys were found guilty of murdering two-year-old James Bulger, opened up a debate that is still continuing into the concept of the age of criminal responsibility. The age of criminal responsibility is currently 10 years old.

References

Barrell, G. R. and Partington, J. A. (1985) *Teachers and The Law*. 6th edn. London: Methuen.

DfEE (1995) Circular 10/95, *Protecting Children from Abuse*. London: HMSO.

DfEE (1997) Education Act. London: HMSO.

DfEE (1998a) Circular 4/98, *Requirements for Initial Teacher Training*. London: HMSO.

DfEE (1998b) Circular 10/98; Section 550A of the Education Act 1996. *The Use of Force to Control or Restrain Pupils*. London: HMSO.

DfES (2001) *Special Educational Needs Code of Practice*. London: DfES.

Home Office (2000) *Race Relations (Amendment) Act*. London: HMSO.

James of Rusholme, Lord (1970) *Report of a Committee of Enquiry into Teacher Education and Training*. (The James Report). London: HMSO.

Local Government Review (1963). *Lyes v Middlesex County Council* (1962).

National Union of Teachers (NUT) (1988) *Towards Equality for Boys and Girls: Guidelines on Countering Sexism in Schools*. London: NUT.

National Union of Teachers (NUT) (1989a) *Job Sharing for Teachers: NUT Guidelines*. London: NUT.

National Union of Teachers (NUT) (1989b) *Anti-Racism in Education: Guidelines Towards a Whole School Policy*. London: NUT.

National Union of Teachers (NUT) (1989c) *Opening Doors: Encouraging Returners Into Teaching as a Career.* London: NUT.

National Union of Teachers (NUT) (1991a) *Fair and Equal – Union Guidelines for Promoting Equal Opportunities in the Appointment and Promotion of Teachers,* 2nd Report. London: NUT.

National Union of Teachers (NUT) (1991b) *Lesbians and Gays in Schools: An Issue for Every Teacher.* London: NUT.

National Union of Teachers (NUT) (1992) *Anti-Racist Curriculum Guidelines.* London: NUT.

National Union of Teachers (NUT) (1995) *Research into the Issuing of Fixed-Term and Temporary Contracts on a Full- or Part-Time Basis with Particular Reference to Women.* London: NUT.

Note: The document referred to does not have a specific title. It is all part of the NUT's occasional but ongoing analysis into the use of temporary and fixed-term contracts. The best title would be: A report of a national survey into teachers' contracts featuring an analysis of the issuing of fixed-term and temporary contracts on a full-time and part-time basis with particular reference to women teachers.

National Union of Teachers (NUT) (2002) *Relearning to Learn. Advice to Teachers New to Teaching Children from Refugee and Asylum-seeking Families.* London: DfES. (Production and distribution funded by the DfES)

Teacher Training Agency (TTA) (2002) Handbook on Guidance on QTS Standards and ITT Requirements. London: DfES.

Trades Union Congress (TUC) (1996) *The Disability Discrimination Act, A TUC Guide.* London: TUC.

Name index

Subject index